Thematic Integration in Board Game Design

Theme is often described as the why of a game. Themes help with rules comprehension by giving reasons for the mechanics. Themes can help set players' expectations for what kind of experiences or emotions the game provides. Themes can also help to create the experience and provide atmosphere to the gameplay.

Thematic Integration in Board Game Design examines the design and integration of theme from the standpoints of technical structure, narrative building, and the design process. This book presents multiple approaches to designing theme as well as developing and replacing themes in existing projects.

The focus is on developing the design skill of mechanical integration of theme rather than developing creative writing skills. Multiple guides and exercises are included that designers can reference at various points in the design process.

Key Features:

- Fills a void in board game design theory by discussing theory-craft relating to theme in board game design
- Presents practical theory for working designers or students
- Focuses on developing the design skill of mechanical integration of theme rather than developing creative writing skills

CRC Press Guides to Tabletop Game Design
Series Editor: Geoffrey Engelstein

Thematic Integration in Board Game Design
Sarah Shipp

Thematic Integration in Board Game Design

Sarah Shipp

CRC Press is an imprint of the
Taylor & Francis Group, an **informa** business

First edition published 2024
by CRC Press
2385 NW Executive Center Drive, Suite 320, Boca Raton FL 33431

and by CRC Press
4 Park Square, Milton Park, Abingdon, Oxon, OX14 4RN

CRC Press is an imprint of Taylor & Francis Group, LLC

Library of Congress Cataloging-in-Publication Data
Names: Shipp, Sarah, author.
Title: Thematic integration in board game design / Sarah Shipp.
Description: Boca Raton, FL : CRC Press, 2024. | Series: CRC Press guides to tabletop game design | Includes bibliographical references and index.
Identifiers: LCCN 2023035975 (print) | LCCN 2023035976 (ebook) | ISBN 9781032592442 (hardback) | ISBN 9781032584058 (paperback) | ISBN 9781003453765 (ebook)
Subjects: LCSH: Board games–Design and construction.
Classification: LCC GV1312. S427 2024 (print) | LCC GV1312 (ebook) | DDC 794–dc23/eng/20230920
LC record available at https://lccn.loc.gov/2023035975
LC ebook record available at https://lccn.loc.gov/2023035976

ISBN: 9781032592442 (hbk)
ISBN: 9781032584058 (pbk)
ISBN: 9781003453765 (ebk)

DOI: 10.1201/9781003453765

Typeset in Minion
by codeMantra

To Geoff, who built the doors, and
to Sen, who opened them.

Contents

Section Three Thematic Design Process

Acknowledgments

THIS BOOK WOULD NOT exist if it were not for those who encouraged me, platformed me, and boosted my blog, particularly Sen-Foong Lim and Jason Perez, who offered me airspace on their respective shows when all they knew about my work was the content of my online comments. I deeply appreciate Suzanne and Chris Zinsli for providing a space dedicated to design theory and accessible to new voices. This book would not be what it is if not for Geoff Engelstein making space for it in his proposal. Thanks to Mark Shipp and Nikolai Voloshko for helping me get through the writing process. Specific thanks are due to Cardboard Edison and Joe Slack from Board Game Design Course for soliciting articles that I later repurposed for this book, to Tabletop Network—in particular Sydney Engelstein, Rikki Tahta, David Thomas, Scott Garbacz, and Luciano Casamajor—for their thoughts on thematic engagement, and to Tabletop Game Designers Guild for providing me with game examples and other sundry assistance.

Author Biography

Sarah Shipp is a freelance theatre technician, board game designer, and blogger. She designed *Deadly Dowagers* and *Monsters Love Vegas!*. Her blog, ShippBoard Games, has received recognition as the best board game design blog of 2022 by Cardboard Edison. In 2021, she presented a talk at the virtual Game Developers Conference on Thematic Resonance. She has also presented at Metatopia Online and Nonepub. In 2023, she became a regular segment contributor to the podcast Ludology. Sarah has an MFA in design and technical production for theatre. She lives in North Texas with her husband, dog, and several dozen mason bees.

ONE

Principles of Theme

CHAPTER 1

What is Theme?

WHAT ARE MECHANICS?

Theme, as a game design term, is almost always discussed in relation to mechanics. Therefore, before an in-depth examination of theme as a concept, it is important to understand what board gamers mean when they say "mechanics."

Hunicke, LeBlanc, and Zubek define mechanics in their paper on MDA as "the various actions, behaviors, and control mechanisms afforded to the player within a game context."[1] Mechanics are not the same as rules. Mechanics are like a car. Rules are the steps you take to turn on the engine and begin driving. The "mechanics" of the car do not allow for flight, and the rules of driving the car do not allow driving on train tracks. Mechanics inevitably have a wider possibility space than rules. However, they are closely related enough that you can view mechanics as structural rules. For example, an auction is a mechanism for acquiring property in the card game *For Sale*, but the rules dictate how much money the players start the game with.

Game design language is still evolving. My personal view is that the terms mechanics and mechanisms function similarly to "people" and "persons." Mechanics describe whole structural systems or categories, whereas mechanisms describe individual structures that happen to coexist. Mechanism is the better term for a single mechanical structure, as a mechanic is a person who works on cars.

DOI: 10.1201/9781003453765-2

COMMON USAGE OF THEME

What do you think of when you hear the word theme? Many times, when people hear the word theme, they think of high school English class and writing essays about what a work of literature means. In this case, theme means the idea that pervades a work. That use of theme is still important to games, notably game criticism. However, it is the less common usage of the word across the English language.

Board game themes use the more common definition of theme, a subject or topic. We see this usage in theme parks and themed parties. If you were invited to a costume party, you might ask, "What's the theme?" This definition and general usage meshes well with how themes were most commonly presented in board games until relatively recently: as window dressing. By this definition, theme is a costume a game wears depending on what the publisher thinks will sell. We are now stuck with the term even as board games move on to more integrated themes.

I am not bothered by the evolution of our expectations for what theme should be. Art changes as our expectations change, but the terms don't always change with it. For example, *deus ex machina* typically refers to a plot device in storytelling, whereas originally it referred to actual machines that revealed representations of the gods in Greek theater.[2] The meanings of words change over time.

Designers occasionally distinguish between setting and theme, although the distinction is really between setting and subject. Setting is the historical, geographical, political, and related contexts that the work exists within. Subject is the topic of the work. Another way of putting it: setting is the window dressing, the background art, and subject is what is actually happening, the emergent narrative. When talking about theme, we might also list a game's thematic genre, such as horror or western. This is different from setting in that setting is specific to a particular game, and thematic genre is a broad generalization of a topic that usually includes other media such as movies. Thematic genre is also different from mechanical genre because a game can be both a worker placement game and a horror game at the same time.

The way we use the term theme does, however, become confusing within the context of games criticism. For one thing, we can't use theme in reference to ideas or meaning in the game while also using it to refer to the subject and setting. I usually default to "subtext" or just "meaning" when discussing the former, but neither term is really a great substitute. Isaac

Shalev suggests using critical theme to talk about the high level themes of a game.[3] On the whole though, games critics seem to be coping without having a separate term.

Where I do think we start to see problems is with designers and gamers who still see theme as window dressing. Because if theme is only window dressing, what right does a game critic have to criticize it? From this perspective, window dressing does not have meaning; a game's art direction is just chosen for marketing reasons and has no impact on the experience of play.[4]

Fundamentally, the argument over whether you should discuss a game's subtext is an argument over the definition of theme as it relates to board games. Is theme merely window dressing that can be changed to any other style of window dressing? Or is theme important both to the emergent narrative of gameplay and the value systems presented by the narrative? Does theme have meaning to game design and the game designer? What is theme?

In all likelihood, your design style is affected by which definition of theme you use.[5] I believe that window dressing, even paired with excellent gameplay, doesn't have the emotional resonance necessary to move us into that future. Besides which, integrated theme sells, and the more it sells, the less patience gamers will have for poorly integrated theme.

A NEW DEFINITION

Theme is important. How we use the term affects how we understand game design and game criticism. The way we use the word theme in the board game hobby is a *term of art*, meaning it has a specific definition to our field that does not exist outside of board games. The more hobby board games develop, the more terms of art we will have. Terms of art are the reason we need board game literature, because we need a standardizing record of what these terms mean. Among other reasons, terms of art are incredibly hard to google.

We have looked at the dictionary definitions of theme—topic and subtext—and drawn a line to how the hobby definition developed from theme-as-topic. We looked at some related terms, setting and subject. Subject closely aligns to the first common definition of theme, a topic. Broadly speaking, subject includes narrative and characters, but narrative or characters are not required in subjects or themes in hobby games. Games depicting real-world systems may not have any characters—perhaps only a single machine and various procedures. While I would say that all themed games contain a story in some form, many game themes do not contain traditional narrative elements. Setting in hobby games not only includes historical, geographical, political, and related contexts, but also tone, mood, and atmosphere. As we'll see below, setting may not always be specified by a game's theme.

There is another element that makes board game themes unique from other forms of art: uncertain outcomes. Games do not play in the same way every time, which affects the narrative of the game. If a theme does not in any way interact with how the game progresses, such as a traditional 52 card deck with superhero court cards that you use to play spades, then the game does not have a theme but a visual art style. The uncertainty of the outcome of a game is what makes the experience of themed games so unique as an art form. The stories found within the subject change from play to play. Board games aren't static, and I feel it is important to reflect that in a good definition of theme.

When we combine all of these elements, we end up with a pretty good definition of theme: ***Theme** in board games is a subject in a setting with an uncertain outcome.* We can flesh out this definition a bit, however, by testing a few assumptions, the main one being "What makes a game themeless?" Let's take a look at each element of the above definition and see what happens if we remove it from a game.

Let's start with the easy element: the uncertain outcome. In order for a theme to be present in a game, it must be tied to gameplay in some way, and games generally do not have scripted endings. Game illustrations can have a subject and a setting, but if they are totally divorced from the momentum of play, then the illustrations function only as an aesthetic style. We see this in classic games that have intellectual properties (or IPs) "pasted" on them in order to appeal to collectors, such as a *Mario* version of *Monopoly*. The more connection that a theme has with the mechanisms, the more thematic a game will feel. However, very few mechanisms need to reflect the theme in order for a theme to feel present. Theme exists on a spectrum that requires at least one point of connectivity in order to function as a theme.

Azul exists on the lower end of this spectrum. *Azul* is a semi-abstract game of choosing and laying plastic tiles that represent the ceramic tiles of Lisbon. It does have several points of connectivity between mechanics and theme: tiles can break, tiles are being placed in a decorative pattern, and the best tile-layer (player) is determined at the end of the game. However, many of the mechanics have no connection to the theme. For example, there is a place on the board that you must fill with tiles of one color before you can add a tile to your facade. The pre-placement area has rows that require between one and five tiles. Why does it take more than one tile to add a tile to your facade? Because the mechanical puzzle demands it. If you must take more tiles than you have room for they can "break" and cost you negative points. The thematic tie-in of tiles breaking gives logic to why you earn negative points. But much of *Azul's* theme appears at the edges of a purely mechanism-driven spatial puzzle.

What if the theme is not tied to the win condition, i.e. how you win the game? Remember, *uncertain outcome* means that the story of the game does not progress in an identical way from game to game. Games often will start with the same setup from play to play but rarely end with the same state. If a meeple took a different pattern of actions one game to the next, its character arc and its world changed. Since the pattern of play is not predetermined before starting a game, I maintain that a theme requires an uncertain outcome, which arises from connectivity to a game's mechanisms. A game will feel themeless if the theme is disconnected from the uncertainty of gameplay. If you win a combat-themed game by receiving points for generating the most resources, a theme might still feel present, but it will feel confused because the goal of the gameplay does not match the theme.

So, theme must connect to the dynamic nature of gameplay. But can theme exist without a setting? It is both difficult and rare for a subject to exist without a setting. It is arguably impossible on a philosophical level. However, we can view setting as what we can know about the game world outside of the central characters and actions. From this angle, I believe that it is possible to have such barely-there settings as to feel nonexistent. For example, *Werewolf* is arguably a subject without a setting. *Werewolf* is a social deduction game that has players voting each day to eliminate one player in the hopes they catch the werewolf before the werewolf can murder all the villagers. This is what we know about the world from playing the basic rules of *Werewolf*: there is a day/night cycle, werewolves exist, and villagers exist. In most versions, a seer (or similar role) also exists. I would argue that isn't enough context to count as a setting. Where does that leave my definition of theme? I would merely add the additional comment that rarely the setting is unspecified. Since setting is often largely provided by/fleshed out by illustration, unspecified settings will be most common in games that have a subject connected to the mechanisms but no (or little) illustration or otherwise specified information about the setting. As previously stated, that's rare in hobby board games, although classic games like chess could also fit in this category. *Werewolf* doesn't feel themeless, but chess does. I suggest that lack of setting contributes to a feeling of themeless-ness, but that games can lack a setting and still feel strongly themed.

Can theme exist without a subject? In short, no. If a setting connects to the mechanisms and components (possibly via illustration), then a subject naturally arises around the actions and goals of the mechanisms, particularly the win condition.[6] So, a purely mechanical game will have no subject or setting, but a game with a specified setting that connects to the mechanics almost certainly has a subject because by connecting a setting to mechanisms a subject will naturally arise.

Does the presence of a subject ensure a theme is present? Surprisingly, there may be subjects that fall outside of what is broadly considered to be theme. The main one is players acting as themselves. If a game has no setting, no characters, and the players act as themselves, I would argue the game effectively has no theme. Many party games, quiz games, and judging games fall into this category. For example, in *Dixit,* a contemplative party game, the only named role is a storyteller. The game has no specified setting. There is one connection point to the role of storyteller: the sentence you must make up on your turn. But because players are literally fulfilling the role as themselves and the action does not mirror real-world storytelling, the connection point seems too tenuous to be able to confidently call it a theme. "Players are 'storytellers' and then we vote" is, at best, a partial theme. Similarly, if the game actions mimic the real-world actions of playing the game too closely, then theme becomes impossible to distinguish from the act of playing the game.[7] Imagine that the theme of the game is that you are playing an abstract board game, but the gameplay is just an abstract board game with no additional worldbuilding. While this game may have a theme, it presents functionally, experientially as having no theme.

But what about our chess example? It has a subject and an uncertain outcome with a connection to mechanics. As I mentioned above, illustration does a lot of the thematic heavy lifting in a game. Chess sets are classically abstracted pieces on a blank grid. In addition, most of the mechanisms do not logically flow from the theme. Chess undeniably has a theme, but that theme doesn't shine through the experience of play.

So, what is a themeless game? Turns out there are several kinds:

- Games with no setting or subject of any kind. (These are typically combinatorial abstract games or classic games.)
- Games with a purported subject and/or setting that has zero connection to the mechanics. (These are similar to the above games, but with illustrations inserted.)
- Games where the subject and setting are so similar to the real-world action of playing the game as to be indistinguishable as a theme. Most often seen when players play as themselves.
- Games that have abstracted the theme so far away as to border on themeless-ness even though they otherwise fit the requirements for having a theme. This is more a perception of themeless-ness than an actual absence of theme.

Using these observations, we can amend our definition of theme:

Theme in hobby board games is a subject in a setting (that may be unspecified) with at least one connection point to the mechanisms which results in an undetermined progression of events at both the mechanical level and the thematic level.

Now that we know what theme is, why should games have a theme? Theme is often described as the *why* of a game. Themes help with rules comprehension by giving reasons for the mechanics. Themes can help set players' expectations for what kind of experiences or emotions the game provides. Themes can also help to create the experience and provide atmosphere to the gameplay. Themes can provide a sense of discovery for players when they uncover subtle ways that the theme informs the mechanics. Themes can encourage creative play and non-victory-related goals.[8]

Exercise 1.1: Pick a theme from one of your designs or a published game. List the subject, setting, and how they connect with the mechanics. You don't have to go into much detail for now. This exercise is to start thinking about theme in these terms.

Exercise 1.2: Pick a published game that feels themeless but isn't an abstract game. Which criteria for themeless-ness does it fit? What could have been done to connect the theme better to the mechanics?

NOTES

1. Robin Hunicke, Marc LeBlanc, and Robert Zubek, "MDA: A Formal Approach to Game Design and Game Research." (AAAI Workshop—Technical Report 1, 2004: 4). MDA is not my preferred framework for game design, but it is the most widely recognized.
2. Oscar G. Brockett and Franklin J. Hildy, *History of the Theatre*, 9th ed. Boston, MA: Allyn and Bacon, 2003: 30–31. Yes, the term is Latin, but it was coined in reference to Greek plays.
3. Isaac Shalev, interview with Donald Dennis and Erik Dewey, *On Board Games*, podcast audio, February 14, 2022. https://sites.libsyn.com/19999/obg-480-one-vision.
4. I suppose the idea that all art has inherent meaning does not enter into the equation because we are talking about art, a very broad term that encompasses all artistic endeavors, and not Art, the sort of work only found in museums. The idea that all art is Art angers a lot of people.
5. For me, theme is an entire topic of study that will help elevate board game design in the decades to come to an indisputable genre of art, with its own museums and college 101 classes and high school interscholastic tournament competitions. That is to say, game design will receive what has been given to every other fine art.
6. For information about how setting is related to mechanisms, see Chapter 8.
7. At least in board games. This is fundamentally what LARPing is.
8. One function of theme is to discourage optimization by encouraging players' imaginations to provide other reasons for performing actions, such as creative expression.

REFERENCES

1. Robin Hunicke, Marc LeBlanc, and Robert Zubek. "MDA: A Formal Approach to Game Design and Game Research." AAAI Workshop - Technical Report 1, 2004: 4.
2. Brockett, Oscar G. and Franklin J. Hildy. *History of the Theatre*, 9th ed. Boston: Allyn and Bacon, 2003.
3. Shalev, Isaac. Interview with Donald Dennis and Erik Dewey. *On Board Games*. Podcast audio. February 14, 2022. https://sites.libsyn.com/19999/obg-480-one-vision.

GAMES REFERENCED

For Sale
Monopoly
Azul
Werewolf
Dixit
Chess

CHAPTER 2

Modes of Thematic Expression

GENERAL TERMS RELATING TO THEME

Theme encompasses the setting, story, and tone or mood of a game. It is expressed via illustration, components, mechanisms, and narrative descriptions. I refer to these items as the elements of a game.

Elements of a game can be motivated or unmotivated. I'm taking these terms from theatrical lighting design.[1] A motivated element is one that has an in-world explanation for existing. Unmotivated elements may not be abstract, but they do not have a clear reason for existing. In theatre, light shining through a window is motivated: we imagine the sun causing the light on the stage, whereas if all of the lights suddenly shift to red, that is unmotivated: we cannot imagine a realistic reason for the light change. Iron ingot components in a game about manufacturing are motivated, whereas the same components are unmotivated in a game about butterflies.

The player pieces in *Monopoly* fall into this category; they are not motivated by the theme of the game. Unmotivated elements are not inherently bad, but they can make a game feel themeless or like the theme is pasted-on, a term popularly used to describe games with themes that don't feel connected to gameplay. Unmotivated elements give an abstract feeling to a game even if the elements are not abstract, such as the pieces in *Monopoly* which are in the shape of common objects. As previously discussed, the

DOI: 10.1201/9781003453765-3

elements of chess are largely not motivated by the theme. Some of the elements, such as the movement patterns, are abstract. Others, such as the piece shapes, have a spectrum of abstraction. But even some pieces that are less abstract are unmotivated by the theme. Castles don't move around in actual warfare. Unmotivated elements make a game feel more abstract than it actually is.

Motivated elements add resonance because they are a form of world-building.[2] What you are saying when you include motivated elements is that these things exist in your game world for a reason. Some unmotivated elements are necessary, such as scoring conditions that can't logically arise from the theme. The trick here is balance. There needs to be enough motivated elements to offset the necessity of including elements that aid rules comprehension and gameplay. If you don't find this balance, the game will either be incomprehensible on a thematic level or the theme will feel pasted-on.[3]

LAYERS OF THEME

Ideally, a game should have consistent theming throughout to produce an engaging thematic experience. Understanding how theme is expressed in the different layers of a game's design can help you identify where your theme may be weak or underdeveloped. You may discover that you skip to layer 3, opt-in elements, in your design and would benefit from spending more time focusing on the thematic expression of core gameplay.

Layer 1: Core Gameplay

A game system is a series of rules and mechanisms that produce an experience even when divorced from theme. This is easiest to see when you play two versions of the same game with a different theme. One popular example is *Schotten Totten* and *Battle Line* by Reiner Knizia.[4] It is possible to build a theme from a complete set of mechanics or even just a core mechanic that enhances the existing experience of a game system. The experience of core gameplay includes mechanisms, rhythm or flow of play, and the tension of decisions. These elements will be present regardless of setting and need to be taken into account when theming a game. Failure to reconcile how a game actually plays with the thematic expression of a game will often create ludonarrative dissonance, a term used when the stated narrative of a game and the gameplay experience are in conflict with each other. Arguably, the core gameplay layer of a design isn't theme, but theme helps shape a specific experience and core gameplay is all about player experience.[5]

Layer 2: Baked-in Thematic Elements

Elements that are baked into a game are thematic elements that cannot be avoided when playing a game. These elements largely define the theme of the game or alternatively create the most ludonarrative dissonance. Baked-in elements include illustration, components, icons, graphics, layout, and terminology.[6] All of these elements define the parameters of the game world because they are so closely tied to the actions of gameplay. You can't help but look at, hold, and manipulate tokens and cards while taking actions. In effectively themed games, the tokens should at bare minimum closely resemble their names, either in shape or illustration.[7] For example, I consistently get the names of the resources wrong in the worker placement, tableau-building game *Everdell*. Two of the resources are pebbles and twigs, which I consistently call stones and sticks. However, because of the effective expression of theme, visually and mechanically, stones and sticks aren't that far off from the intended pebbles and twigs. If players are consistently referring to your resources by their color names, the theming is probably not effective.

Cubes are inherently more difficult to incorporate thematically because nothing about them, except color, helps reinforce the theme. Games that use cubes to represent cargo crates manage to subvert this. Another example of slightly less abstract cube usage is *Century: Spice Road*, a resource upgrading, contract fulfillment game, which uses cubes to represent spices. In *Century: Spice Road*, the different colors of cube correspond to different colors of spice. Piles of cubes can be imagined as somewhat clumped piles of spices.

Layer 3: Opt-in Thematic Elements

Opt-in elements are elements that can be ignored during gameplay. This includes "flavor" text on cards, narrative text found in the rulebook, narrative or dialogue breaks that interrupt play, additional lore or components located in companion products, and meta-play, here used to mean play that occurs outside of what the rules instruct. The difference between opt-in elements and baked-in elements is that opt-in elements invariably distract from or break the flow of gameplay. That doesn't mean they are inherently bad, but it does help explain why so many players choose to ignore flavor text. These elements exist for the players who want to engage with them and should enhance the overall play experience for those players by working with the other layers and not against them.

Meta-play on the thematic side of play includes role-play, describing your character's reactions, silly voices, etc.[8] Meta-play is difficult to design for. Some notable games that encourage meta-play are *Sheriff of Nottingham* and *Gloom*. *Sheriff of Nottingham* is a game of taking goods through customs. The rules require players to speak aloud the composition of the goods they are trying to take to market, with the expectation that players will frequently lie about which goods they have. Since players are already speaking and performing actions as a single character in the game, role-play arises naturally among players who are comfortable with this sort of meta-play. Not all players wish to engage in meta-play, and games will often be composed of a mixed group of players, some who will opt-in and some who won't. *Gloom* is a card game about terrible things happening to a family in a gothic cartoon-like setting. *Gloom* doesn't have a structure that encourages role-play the way that *Sheriff* does. Instead, the flavor text and card play of *Gloom* encourage players to elaborate on events as a form of guided storytelling. Players who don't connect with the meta-play of *Gloom* seem to rate the game much lower than players who do. The fun of the game is not the mechanisms but the stories that arise from the execution of gameplay.

The important thing to know about this level is that opt-in elements cannot be where your theme begins and ends. The mechanisms of both the games mentioned here still provide an integrated thematic experience in addition to a rich opt-in experience. Opt-in elements should be the final touches on a game that feels thematic even when players ignore those elements.

Baked-in elements are necessary to thematic design. Opt-in elements can enrich the experience of play or can serve as distractions. Designers often focus their worldbuilding around opt-in elements while not putting enough focus on how the baked-in elements tell the story of the game on the table.

KNITTED AND LAYERED THEMES

Chapter 1 states that an art style is not enough to qualify as a game's theme. There must be at least one connection point to the mechanics. In the remainder of this chapter, I want to look at the spectrum of connectivity between theme and mechanisms.

The term "pasted-on theme" is largely derogatory, although it's used frequently for otherwise well-respected games. I propose two terms to replace it, knitted and layered. Layered themes are developed separately from the mechanisms, then layered on top of them. Layered is the direct replacement of pasted-on, but lacks the derogatory tone. A layered theme has connection points to the mechanics, but they often feel inorganic. The emotional experiences of the theme and the mechanics may feel like two separate experiences. This can be seen with games that completely develop mechanisms before finding a theme, but could also be found in games with a completed theme that has mechanisms layered on top of it, such as mass market games that use movie IPs. Or the designer could simply develop both in parallel without much concern for how they intersect.

Layered themes will often have some baked-in thematic elements (such as resource tokens) and some written lore,[9] but will usually not have mechanisms that match the experience of the theme. Actions will be a mixture of thematic actions and mechanical actions.[10] Often, the layout of the board will lack any connection to the theme. The experience of play will rely heavily on the mechanics, sometimes feeling out of step with the theme. A layered theme is still a theme, but players may describe the game as "not thematic." Layered themes are not inherently bad, but should be designed and presented intentionally so as not to give players the impression that they will have a thematic experience that is not present in the game.

Love Letter is an example of a game with a layered theme. In *Love Letter*, characters are trying to get a letter to the Princess. Mechanically, players are trying to deduce who other players are and eliminate them through card play. What players are doing bears little resemblance to the theme of the game. I'll discuss *Love Letter* more in Chapter 5 to address how the game could have better integrated the theme.

A knitted theme has many connection points between theme and mechanics. Knitted themes are more likely to have been developed simultaneously alongside the mechanics of a game. Because of how integrated the theme and mechanics are, a knitted theme will be difficult to retheme without changing the design of some of the mechanics. Knitted themes present a more unified experience. However, knitted themes are not inherently immersive.[11] Mechanic-thematic integration revolves around how well the mechanics and theme are connected, not around the type of experience it provides. A game may be immersive because of the narrative but have layered mechanics or a "loosely" knitted theme where only some of the mechanics are knitted but some are not. Indeed, many American style (or Ameritrash) games could be categorized as loosely knit, with the bulk of the theme coming from illustration, narrative, or the player's prior knowledge of the IP.

Whether or not a game has a tightly knitted theme may be somewhat subjective. The mechanics need to be largely motivated by the theme and provide a similar emotional experience as the theme. These terms aren't meant to judge how accurately the mechanics simulate the theme, merely the interconnectedness of theme and mechanics. Any immersion or simulation or aligned emotional experience may be the result of a tightly knitted theme but knitted themes lend themselves to many different sorts of play experiences, including German or European style (also called Euro) games.

Examples of knitted themes include *Guillotine* and *Everdell. Guillotine* is a small box card game with a similar complexity to *Love Letter.* In *Guillotine*, players are rearranging nobles in a line for execution during the French Revolution. Unlike in *Love Letter*, the characters on the cards and the mechanics of play feel connected to the theme of the game. Nevertheless, *Guillotine* has only a loosely knitted theme. Players are more concerned with gaining points than an overarching story of the theme. When a game puts a significant amount of emphasis on acquiring components with assigned numeric values in order to win, the theme will usually take a back seat to strategic math. In games like *Everdell*, the goal of gaining the most points gets obscured by other mechanical and thematic desires when playing the game. Thematically, players may want to have houses for all their townsfolk or achieve certain goals or events because of the narrative elements these provide, even if doing so is less optimized for winning.

The world of the game exists from setup until final scoring. The theme should enhance what happens in that period of time. Lore text alone will not make your game thematic. Building your theme from the core layer outwards ensures that your theme will be knitted with your mechanics.

THEMATIC ACTIONS

In order to have a well-knitted theme, you must have a thematically motivated core gameplay. Games, however, will always have some level of abstraction. Keeping a balance of thematic and abstract mechanics is important. However, thematic implementation is not a binary state.

There are five degrees of how thematic an action can be that can exist in a game: mechanical, associated, metaphoric, simulative, and literal.

Mechanisms are units of play that have widely varying sizes. A mechanism may be a piece of an action or may be a way of describing the entire flow of a game. For instance, "engine building" is descriptive of how a game is structured; you can't determine if an unfamiliar game is an engine builder by looking at only one action. Actions are player-driven changes to a play-state that occur once a game has begun and before a game ends, i.e. setup and end game scoring are not counted as actions.

Actions are more uniform in length and usually involve the player doing a single thing.[12] When working on theming a game, thematic actions are an easier place to start than thematic mechanisms. Many mechanisms—deck building, drafting, etc.—are difficult to tie into a theme. You can match the experiences or emotions of the theme with those mechanisms to create a more unified experience, but in this section, I'm going to be looking at types of actions so that we can better understand how theme presents at a gameplay level.[13]

The first two actions could be described as *utilitarian actions*. They move gameplay forward without adding to the thematic experience.

- **Mechanical actions** are the unthemed actions of a game. Almost every game will have some of these. Examples include drawing a card or scoring a victory point. In a themed game, these actions are necessary to the function of play but should recede to the background as much as possible. Don't be afraid to put mechanical actions into a thematic game but do so sparingly.

- **Associated actions** reinforce the logic of the theme but do not relate mechanically or experientially to the theme. In other words, associated actions are labeled thematically and that's where the theme ends. Let's imagine a game with actions themed around kicking a ball into a goal. An action that moves a cube to indicate whether or not you have kicked on your turn would be an associated action. The action is associated with the theme (kicking) but only very tangentially. Just like mechanical actions, some associated actions may be necessary for the function of play.

The next three action types fall under the umbrella of *evocative actions*. They evoke the theme of the game. Thematic experiences rely largely on evocative actions. However, you have options in how you choose to evoke your theme.

- **Metaphoric actions** evoke similar experiences, emotions, or idioms as the theme. This category of action—and this whole system as a result—was inspired by Geoffrey Engelstein's discussion of how themes present as metaphors in gameplay.[14] In our ball-kicking game, rolling a die and succeeding in scoring a goal on a high number would be a metaphoric action. The experience of a successful role mimics the experience of a successful kick, but does not simulate physical kicking. Metaphoric actions may act as emotional simulations. They can also use idiomatic gaming concepts, such as our correlation of high rolls with success.
- **Simulative actions** simulate physical aspects of the theme. There are many types of simulations, but for our purposes, simulative actions mimic real-world physical events. The action does not, or not just, mirror the emotions of the theme, but the physical action imagined by the theme. Flicking a disc onto a circle simulates kicking a ball in a way that rolling a die does not (unless you are rolling the die toward a goal). There are going to be cases where you could argue either way over what is simulative and what is metaphoric or even how I define the difference. These categories are intended to help expand our understanding of what theme is and how it presents in gameplay.
- **Literal actions** are an actual performance of the theme by the players. Literal actions are one step beyond simulative. A literal action would be kicking a ball. In *MonsDRAWsity*, players are police sketch artists thematically. In the game, they *literally* produce sketches based on descriptions provided by a "witness." If the theme of a game was to be "playing a game," then all mechanical actions would be literal actions.

Most games have a mixture of action types. I think the most important distinction is understanding the difference between associated actions and the evocative action umbrella. A game that is mostly made up of associated actions will feel themeless to players. A well-knitted theme should have a healthy dose of evocative actions. Evocative actions can do a lot of the heavy-lifting of world building from the inside out.

Theme in board games is expressed in many different ways and to different degrees. Adding terms like motivated, baked-in, opt-in, knitted, layered, associated action, metaphoric action, and literal action can help designers think about how they express theme in their own designs.

Exercise 2.1: Pick a published game with a theme. Which elements are motivated by the theme and which are unmotivated? How could the unmotivated elements have been changed to be motivated by the theme?

Exercise 2.2: Pick one of your designs or a published game. Describe the elements that are part of the core gameplay layer, the baked-in layer, and the opt-in layer. Go into as much detail and include as many elements as you can.

Exercise 2.3: List five published games with layered themes. What do these games have in common? List five published games with knitted themes. What do they have in common?

Exercise 2.4: Pick one of your designs or a published game. List every action in the game and what kind of action type it is.

NOTES

1. Richard Pilbrow, *Stage Lighting Design: The Art, The Craft, The Life*. Hollywood, CA: Design Press, 2008: 25.
2. Resonance is discussed in Chapter 11. World-building is addressed in Chapter 4.
3. This balance is discussed in depth in Chapter 4, in the section discussing the game world vs. the game state.
4. The BoardGameGeek.com page for *Schotten Totten* says it reimplements *East-West* and *The Fifth Column* and is reimplemented by *Los Banditos*, *Battle Line*, *Battle Line: Medieval*, *Knights Poker*, and *Schotten Totten 2*. In case you wondered how extreme retheming can get.
5. This idea is explored more in the second half of Chapter 3.
6. Terminology sits on the cusp between baked-in and opt-in, because so many terms are ignored in favor of color or shape names. I would argue that is the result of bad theme implementation, however.
7. It would be better for the tokens to be used mechanically in intuitive ways that reflect their theming. Especially in games with made-up resources.
8. Meta-play on the strategic side of play will be discussed more in Chapter 6 in the context of social leveraging.
9. Lore that has no impact on gameplay is popularly termed "fluff."
10. These action types are discussed later in this chapter.

11. Immersion is not expressly discussed in this book. My thoughts on immersion align with the introduction to *In Game: From Immersion to Incorporation* by Gordon Calleja. He divides immersion into two categories: absorption and transportation. Cambridge, MA: MIT Press, 2011.
12. Chapter 4 will discuss mechanical categories of actions in depth.
13. Chapter 3 covers larger mechanical structures and their thematic considerations.
14. Geoffrey Engelstein, interview with Gil Hova and Sen-Foong Lim, *Ludology*, podcast audio, February 20, 2022, https://ludology.libsyn.com/ludology-268-pinball-wizard.

REFERENCES

1. Pilbrow, Richard. *Stage Lighting Design: The Art, The Craft, The Life.* Hollywood, CA: Design Press, 2008.
2. Calleja, Gordon. *In Game: From Immersion to Incorporation.* Cambridge, MA: MIT Press, 2011.
3. Engelstein, Geoffrey. Interview with Gil Hova and Sen-Foong Lim. Ludology. Podcast audio. February 20, 2022. https://ludology.libsyn.com/ludology-268-pinball-wizard.

GAMES REFERENCED

Monopoly
Schotten Totten
Battle Line
Everdell
Century: Spice Road
Gloom
Sheriff of Nottingham
Love Letter
Guillotine
MonsDRAWsity

CHAPTER 3

Thematically Structuring Games

THEMES CAN SUGGEST THE mechanical structures of games and structures can suggest themes. This chapter covers the mechanical possibilities present in themes and the thematic possibilities present in mechanisms through the lens of how games are structured.

This chapter presents two modes of game structure, metaphors and mechanical structure categories. Which approach you prefer will depend on your personal process as a designer. Both are merely different ways of thinking about the structure of thematic design. I use both in my design process; they are not mutually exclusive.

CENTRAL THEMATIC METAPHORS

Theme is most often and most effectively presented in game mechanics as a metaphor.[1] Strong metaphors in game design can bring a theme to life. Metaphors do not need to be visually expressed, but metaphors with a visual component add richness and verisimilitude to the gameplay experience. Metaphors express the logic of the game rules and convey the emotion of the theme. Metaphoric mechanics differ from metaphoric actions in that metaphoric mechanics are broader concepts that can be applied to the game as a structural whole as opposed to the action-unit. A metaphoric mechanic usually combines a mechanism, components, and theme: "Using X component in Y mechanism, players will metaphorically experience Z theme."

DOI: 10.1201/9781003453765-4

One way I like to approach a new design is to focus the early design process around a central thematic metaphor applied to a single mechanism. A design should have only one central metaphor, but that metaphor can develop and become more complex as the game develops. A central thematic metaphor is the non-negotiable design element, meaning that you can change every last mechanism, but as long as the new mechanisms express the same core idea and feeling then you are still making the same game you set out to make.

Central thematic metaphors work best when mechanically expressed although they can begin as component-based metaphors. A strong metaphor permeates the design process and filters into the mechanisms, even if the original metaphoric concept was originally component-based rather than mechanism-based. Central metaphors are useful when determining how pieces move, the rhythm of play, and the amount of player interaction. Incorporating movement, timing, and/or player interaction with the central metaphor will deepen the player's experience of the theme, provided the central metaphor is closely aligned with the stated theme of the game.

A central thematic metaphor is similar but distinct from the concept of "designing for the intended player experience." You can do both at once, however. Intended experience is how you want your players to feel while they play your game. A central metaphor is a more cognitive expression of an idea that ties strongly to an object or activity. For example, the central metaphor of the cooperative game *Paleo* is the struggle for survival as primitive humans expressed via the player decks which reveal random challenges that the players must navigate. The experience of play in *Paleo* encompasses the sense of urgency, stress, and relief players feel as they encounter the central metaphor of survival via the game mechanics. The metaphor focuses on the mechanisms and components of gameplay, and the intended experience arises from the act of play. If the metaphor and the play experience are not tonally consistent, either or both can be adjusted or changed, depending on your vision for the game. I am more likely to change my intended experience than my central metaphor as the game develops, because, for me, the metaphor is where the game lives.

Why not focus on the intended experience instead of designing metaphors? It is easier to make a descriptive metaphor central to gameplay than it is to make an emotion central to gameplay. For one thing, not every player will experience the same emotions when playing a game.

Additionally, action verbs and concrete objects are easier to generate ideas around than emotions. "I want players to feel urgency" is good to include in your design vision, but "I want players to struggle for survival in prehistoric Europe" is much more fertile ground for guiding thematic design decisions. The emotion of an intended experience acts more as a guidepost as the game develops. You can check the latest version of your game against how you intend it to feel using playtester feedback. Keep in mind, however, that it is possible for you to make the game more in line with the intended experience while also making it less thematic. The central thematic metaphor helps keep the theme present as the game develops. If a game needs changes that move it away from the theme, you could look at changing the theme in order to maintain a strong mechanical metaphor.

As the saying goes, write what you know. It is easier to ground your theme in a metaphor if you are familiar with that theme already. Otherwise, research is your best friend. When starting a new design, research themes you are interested in.[2] Look for an aspect of your chosen theme that suggests some element of gameplay. From there, distill a central thematic metaphor and intended player experience. That's essentially a design vision, and if you write it down, you have a design vision statement that you can reference throughout the design process. A design vision statement could be worded as "I want players to experience X emotion through Y metaphor." For example, "I want players to experience the wonder of traveling by zeppelin through the metaphor of a conveyor belt board that provides the illusion of traveling great distances without taking up the entire table" could be the design vision statement for the board game *Solenia*. Here, wonder is the intended experience, and traveling large distances by zeppelin via a conveyor belt mechanism is the metaphor. Design vision statements are used as guideposts throughout the design process. They may need to be reevaluated if your concept develops in a more interesting direction, at which point you should devise a new or more detailed design vision statement.

MECHANICAL GAME STRUCTURES

Not every design starts with a central metaphor. Many design ideas start with general mechanical concepts that later incorporate theme. It does not matter if you start a design theme-first or mechanics-first, because you can knit theme to mechanics regardless of at which point you start. One of the best ways to connect theme to an existing game idea early on is to consider the mechanical structure of the game and what types of themes fit easily within that structure.

Have you ever noticed that some thematic genres tend to get paired with the same mechanics over and over? There is a reason that most dungeon crawlers look and feel similar. Certain mechanical game structures lend themselves to certain types of stories. Understanding how high-level structure impacts storytelling can help you design themes that feel organic to a game.

In this section, I outline six categories, but those categories can be combined in different ways to produce distinct, interesting games. I divide these categories less on how mechanically distinct they are from one another and more on how they feel and what types of themes fit well with them, especially when looking at the first two categories. Any themes and mechanisms listed are just common ones to get you started and should not limit you from exploring other ideas that might fit with the experience of play. The associated diagrams are to help visualize the differences between the structures.

Puzzles

This category could potentially be divided into two categories: puzzle-solving structures with a set of single answers and efficiency puzzles that could have multiple right answers. I've lumped them together because I find that figuring out the best/right answer feels cognitively similar across multiple genres. Single solution puzzle structure encompasses logic puzzles, deduction, code-breaking, and other similar mechanical structures. Puzzle-solving often occurs in cooperative or solo games. Efficiency puzzle structures include bingo-style mechanisms and time or resource management where the goal is to perform actions more efficiently than other players. Efficiency puzzles are most prevalent in low-interaction, competitive games. However, these two substructures can be found in the same game, such as *Project L*, a game about acquiring the polyomino pieces you need through engine-building actions in order to create specific shapes (Figures 3.1 and 3.2).

Puzzle-solving structures lend themselves to mystery stories, detective stories, and horror stories, but also stories about hackers, cryptographers, and code-breakers. Escape room style games—such as the *Exit* or *Unlock* series—are clearly puzzle-solving, but also any game with specific objectives such as the pattern matching game *ROVE: Results-Oriented Versatile*

FIGURE 3.1 A puzzle-solving structure. The line represents a player's progress through the game. The triangle is the game objective. The circles represent actions available to a player. In puzzle-solving structures, puzzles must be completed in order for the player to progress, represented by locks.

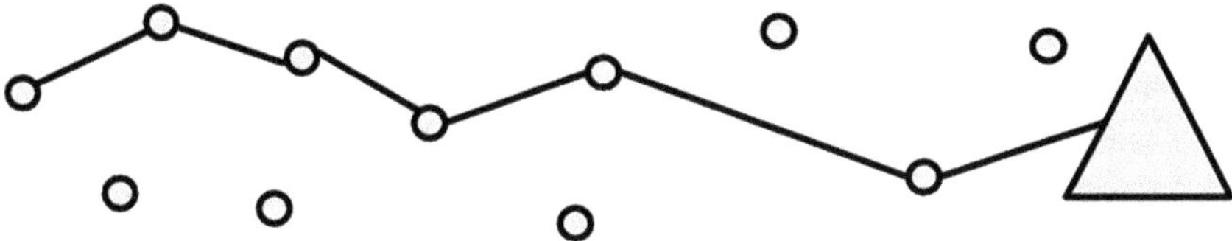

FIGURE 3.2 An efficiency puzzle structure. The lines represent a player's progress through the game. The triangle is the game objective. The circles represent actions available to a player. The player must choose the most efficient path out of a variety of actions.

Explorer. In *ROVE*, the player uses various movement rules to create patterns that match the target cards. Efficiency puzzles are frequently structured around expanding power and options, diminishing choices, or sometimes both. While most gamers associate rules-heavy Euro games with efficiency puzzles, efficiency is also the hallmark of the roll-and-write genre. An example of a roll-and-write game with an expanding power arc is *Fleet: The Dice Game.* As you roll dice and tick off boxes, you unlock abilities that increase the value of future turns. An example of a roll-and-write game with sharply diminishing choices is the *Railroad Ink* series of games. Over the course of six or seven rounds, players fill in routes on personal boards. By the last few turns, players are locked in to what dice they can use and may have to start a route they can't finish when a track they don't want is rolled. An example of a roll-and-write game that has both expanding power and diminishing choices is the *Super Skill Pinball* series of games, in which players mark off sections of a pinball table as they roll dice and gradually unlock powers while trying to keep their "ball" in play for as long as possible.

Try to match your theme to the dynamics present in the puzzle. Stories about players trying to outlast what the game throws at them could lean into either substructure or both. Themes that don't benefit from a feeling of "running out of time" will fail to tap into the full potential of puzzle-solving structures.

Cycles

On the surface, cycles can look a lot like efficiency puzzles, but I think they lend themselves to very different stories. Cyclical structures contain repeating events that lead into one another. Cyclical structures rely heavily on timing, but in a vastly different way from puzzle-solving structures. Cycles demand that you tactically take advantage of certain game states at just the right moment, but may not lead to the "running out of time" feeling of puzzle-solving structures. Because events will recur again and again, cyclical games feel less hurried and pressured. However, they still require an emphasis on efficiency to play well. Traits of cyclical structures include intermittent scoring, multiple phases, set collection, and engine building (Figure 3.3).

Cycles may be player dependent like the seasons in *Everdell,* which advance for each player only when they have finished with the previous season, or they may be global like the ages in *7 Wonders,* which occur at the same time for all players. Cycles can occur on a player's turn or over the course of multiple turns, as in *Everdell* and *7 Wonders.* A more complex version of cycles can be found in *Succulent. Succulent* cycles between two sub-cycles on a player's turn: players may either take tiles or play one on the board, and players have the option to score cards as a part of their turn. The cycle in *Succulent* is first a choice of take or play tiles, then a choice to score or not score. In practice, players won't be able to score every round and may not want to score low value cards when they are able but instead save resources for higher value cards. So the scoring cycle occurs intermittently, whereas the tile cycle occurs every turn, but players control which part of the tile cycle they trigger.

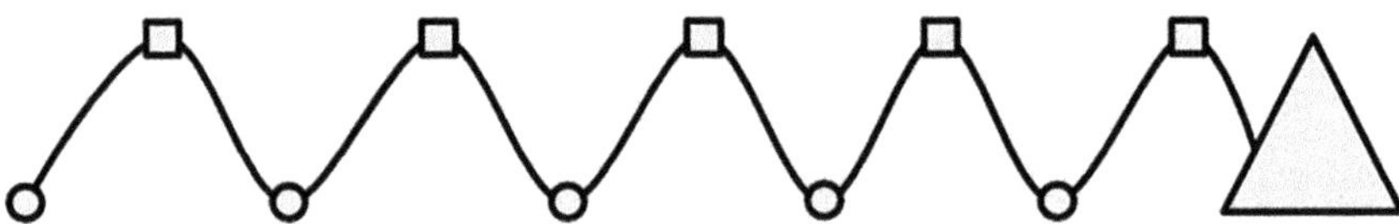

FIGURE 3.3 A cyclical game structure. The actions at the bottom of the wave are all one type of action and the actions at the top of the wave are a different type of action, represented by squares. Players progress through the game via alternating types of actions.

Keep in mind that a game could be both an efficiency puzzle and cyclical. Pick-up-and-deliver and rondels are mechanisms that are often found in efficiency-focused games, but are very cyclical in nature. I wouldn't describe a game with two distinctly different halves as cyclical, although either or both halves could be cyclical in structure. Cyclical structure lends itself to themes such as natural systems (for example, life cycles or weather), industrial systems, generational storytelling, and cooking. Any theme that lends itself to templates or formulas—especially if a character might repeat a process multiple times in a row—works well in a cyclical game. Cyclical structures are my favorite to design in.

Race to Finish

First past the post can refer to victory conditions or to other goals within a game or cycle or phase. Race to finish structure focuses on rewarding the player who meets a requirement first. Alternatively, race to finish structures can be used to qualify players for scoring, a form of end game player elimination. One hallmark of race to finish games is that the momentum of the game is strongly focused on the objective or win condition.[3] Race to finish structures can be a layer added to other structures to increase the tension of gameplay. On its own, this structure often utilizes more randomness than other structures—with the exception of open conflict. Race to finish mechanics include dice-rolling, betting, ladder climbing, headwinds and tailwinds, and pawn movement mechanics. Themes that mesh well include competitions or contests, which of course includes actual races, such as *Heat: Pedal to the Metal.* If a theme emphasizes speed, race to finish is a good go-to structure. Cooperative games may have a race to finish oriented around a race against time or against the game AI, such as in *Pandemic* where players are racing against the game to cure diseases (Figure 3.4).

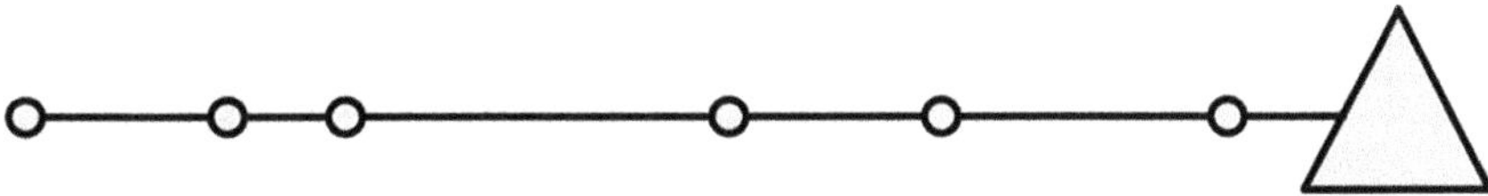

FIGURE 3.4 A race to finish structure. All the actions are the same general type and lead to straightforward progress. However, the amount of progress can vary from action to action.

Race to Fill

Race to fill structure is a race to expand or exploit. This structure pairs well with other structures that emphasize efficiency. Race to fill differs from race to finish in that the player who gets somewhere first may not be the winner but rather the player who does the most.[4] This structure includes mechanisms such as area control, area majority, tile laying, city building, and set collection. *Carcassonne* combines tile laying and area majority for a simple introduction to race to fill, where players are placing tiles and claiming regions with meeples. Race to fill games create tension through scarcity of resources or space. Pick-up-and-deliver games can combine race to fill with race to finish and/or cyclical structure. Race to fill is often cyclical, but the addition of race to fill adds tension to cyclical games. For example, *Roam* is an area majority game that is played out on cards that refill whenever a player has completed a card, making it more cyclical than most area majority games. Common themes in this structure include city planning, forest planting, territory conquest, exploration, and order fulfillment (such as a short order cook) (Figure 3.5).

Open Conflict

Open conflict structures center on players giving and receiving damage from other players and/or the game. These are pretty much always fighting games although damage could be to anything, not just health. The defining aspect of open conflict is that objectives and sides are known by all players; damage is not done in secret. Open conflict games often have player elimination, alliances, and leveling up mechanics. Most "take that" mechanics are forms of open conflict.[5] Common themes are war, survival, and adventuring/dungeon-crawling. Open conflict can be cyclical, especially when using leveling up mechanisms or in sports-themed games. The danger of

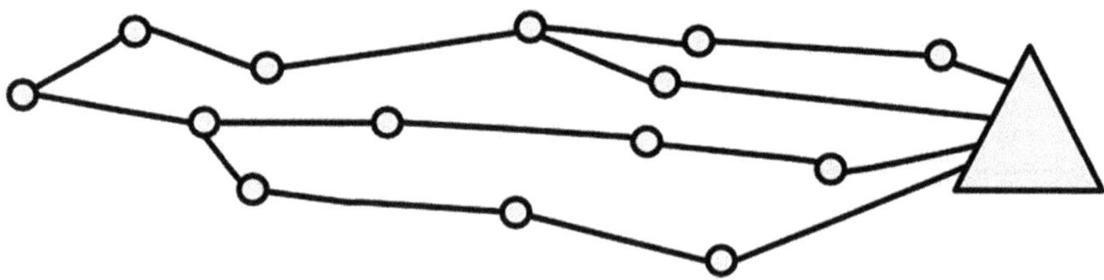

FIGURE 3.5 A race to fill structure. Player progress branches out in multiple directions, but all progress feeds into the overall objective.

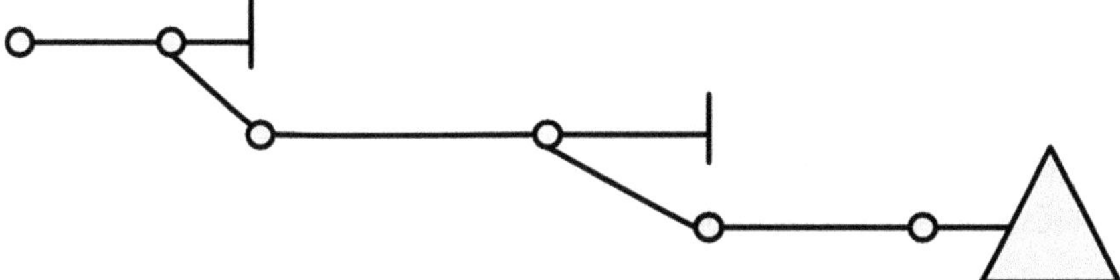

FIGURE 3.6 An open conflict structure. The vertical lines represent a failure to progress due to an opponent's actions. This could be the elimination of a unit or an effective blockade of a territory. The player must then change tactics in order to progress toward the objective.

having open conflict as only one aspect of the game is that it will often feel like a separate mini game that interrupts the flow of the overall game. *Risk* is a classic example of an open conflict game (Figure 3.6).

Covert Conflict

Covert conflict structures involve secrets: secret objectives, secret roles, secret teams, hidden movement, or some combination of the above. Covert conflict also has player elimination, but often via vote instead of damage. In addition to player elimination and voting, common mechanisms include negotiation, bluffing, trading/deal-making, deduction, and traitors. Covert conflict games often fall in the party game adjacent category (social deduction, etc.), but there have been larger games with an emphasis on covert conflict. Larger/heavier games are likely to combine covert conflict with other structures, especially open conflict. *Fury of Dracula* is a hidden movement game where most of the players are trying to hunt down and stop Dracula, played by one of the players. However, whenever Dracula or another vampire is discovered by the hunter players, the game switches to open conflict mechanisms. *Bang!* is an example of a small game that blends open and covert conflict. Players have hidden roles, which are revealed as players are eliminated through open conflict. Themes commonly paired with covert conflict are spying and diplomacy. Covert conflict usually contains a high social factor in gameplay in the form of speculation, discussion, and deal-making; as a result, the well-integrated themes of such games usually center on who the characters are and their relationships both mechanically and thematically (Figure 3.7).

FIGURE 3.7 A covert conflict structure. In this example, a player is caught and eliminated from the game before reaching the objective.

Special Hybrids: Pivot Points

Sometimes games have two distinct halves or phases, such as *Bosk,* which has players grow trees in the first half of the game then scatter leaves in the second half. These halves may have different structures, but the game controls when they occur. Other times, games have player-controlled pivots. Pivot points allow a game arc to have a distinct rising-action-pivot-falling-action arc. There are two very common pivot point structures: "Grab the Treasure and Run" and "Reaping What You Sow." In "grab the treasure and run," the rising action is acquiring as many point-scoring items as possible (usually an efficiency puzzle). After the pivot, players must move as quickly as possible to the zone that will allow them to score their loot (race to finish). These games usually center push your luck mechanics. The board game *Clank!* literally has players grabbing as much treasure as possible before racing to escape the dragon's lair. In "reaping what you sow," the rising action is building up resources or an engine and the falling action is cashing in on your hard work. Deck builders and other engine building mechanics employ this type of pivot. The card game *Dominion* features a pivot when players stop trying to build up their deck "engines" and start trying to turn their cards into points. I would like to see more types of pivot points explored. A pivot point can make the story of a game come alive because its structure closely resembles narrative structure. Even when not well-integrated with theme, pivot points add excitement to gameplay (Figure 3.8).

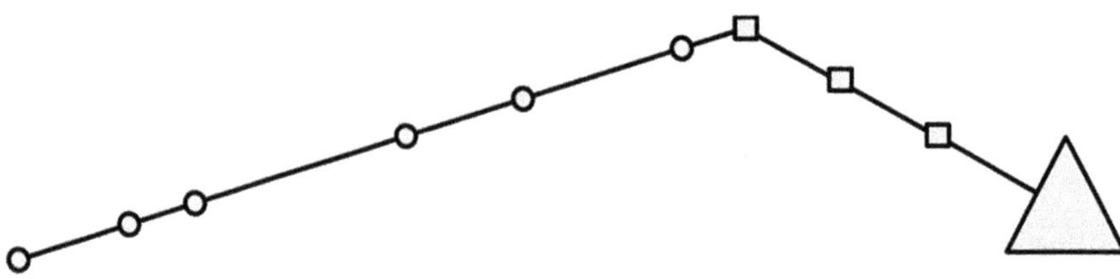

FIGURE 3.8 A simplified pivot point structure. Actions in the early game lead to a pivot to different actions in the late game.

Mechanisms suggest themes by their rhythm and structure and ability to create tension/excitement. Mechanisms also tend to gravitate to certain game structures. There is a reason player elimination feels wrong in an efficiency game. Themes might feel pasted-on if they aren't a good match for the game structure. Analyze the games you have designed. What structures did you use? What structure are you drawn to most? I tend to design in the same structures as the games I enjoy playing. Because I enjoy designing cyclical games (which I think is the coziest structure), I tend to brainstorm game ideas around themes that employ templates, like cooking from a recipe. When starting a new design, you could brainstorm by combining two structures then looking at what themes and mechanisms would work well together within those structures.

Design vision statements can include structure and intended experience instead of a metaphor. Which you use depends on how you develop an early idea. You may know right away that you want an exciting open conflict game, but you may be months into development before you come up with a mechanism that serves as a metaphor for the theme.

Exercise 3.1: Pick one of your designs or a published game. What is the central thematic metaphor? How would the theme of the game change if the metaphor changed?

Exercise 3.2: Create a design vision statement for one of your designs that is based on the central metaphor of the theme.

Exercise 3.3: Make a list of your designs that made it to the playtesting stage. What types of structures do they have? Do those structures make sense with the themes? Do you have a favorite structure that appears in many of your designs?

NOTES

1. I use the term metaphor because board games rarely act as faithful simulations, but instead abstract concepts in an artistic way.
2. Research is discussed in Chapter 10.
3. For a much more detailed examination of the mechanics of this structure, the blog Games Precipice has an in-depth post about late game structures (Alex Harkey, "Late Game Structure—Objectives and Victory Conditions." *Games Precipice* (blog), November 13, 2018. https://www.gamesprecipice.com/objectives/?fbclid=IwAR22I64WR2wnTrMY0iEETsByiBgwq7cqAqEhZfFSOe-xHa9qOAcM-XJQdKs.) I should note that race to finish is either about the whole of the game or a goal within the game, whereas "go the fastest" in the post from Games Precipice is about the endgame state.

4. Similar to "go the farthest" in the article from *Games Precipice* referenced previously. However, the same caveats apply that race to fill can be a minor goal, whereas "go the farthest" refers to the endgame.
5. "Take that" is a term that is used for typically non-thematic mechanics that negatively affect an opposing player.

REFERENCE

1. Harkey, Alex. "Late Game Structure-Objectives and Victory Conditions." *Games Precipice* (blog), November 13, 2018. https://www.gamesprecipice.com/objectives/?fbclid=IwAR22I64WR2wnTrMY0iEETsByiBgwq7cqAqEhZfFSOe-xHa9qOAcM-XJQdKs.

GAMES REFERENCED

Paleo
Solenia
Project L
Exit series
Unlock series
ROVE: Results-Oriented Versatile Explorer
Fleet: The Dice Game
Railroad Ink series
Super Skill Pinball series
Everdell
7 Wonders
Succulent
Heat: Pedal to the Metal
Pandemic
Carcassonne
Roam
Risk
Fury of Dracula
Bang!
Book
Clank!
Dominion

TWO

Theme-Building

CHAPTER 4

Connecting Story to Gameplay

WHEN DESIGNERS DISCUSS BUILDING out their themes, they often do so using the term worldbuilding. Worldbuilding refers to the background story elements and setting that inform what happens in your story. Worldbuilding is often expressed through opt-in elements, such as lore booklets. In order to differentiate the act of crafting the story of what happens during gameplay from the creation of a larger lore, I use the term theme-building. Theme-building is crafting the story within the core gameplay and baked-in elements of the game.

The next five chapters will look at the components of theme-building, subject and setting, from an in-game narrative perspective. Subject can be further broken down into narrative or plot and characters, although these concepts are interwoven. Chapter 5 will cover elements related to narrative. Chapters 6 and 7 cover characters. Chapter 8 discusses setting. Chapter 9 provides a quick reference guide for theme-building.

This chapter introduces foundational concepts that we will use to build on as we discuss narrative, characters, and setting. The first section explores how goals and obstacles combine to produce conflict. The second section looks at how types of mechanical actions can express thematic goals. The third section begins to identify areas of design that are important to theme vs. areas where theme should be de-emphasized or avoided.

DOI: 10.1201/9781003453765-6

GOALS, OBSTACLES, AND CONFLICT

Chapter 3 covered initial structural elements around which a theme can be built. Once you have a metaphor and general mechanical structure, it is time to start thinking about the plot. In order to have a plot, you need to have some kind of conflict. Conflict exists when something or someone (i.e. an obstacle) stands between you and your goal. Any type of obstacle will create conflict. Conflict creates tension and urgency. Overcoming conflict creates feelings of achievement and satisfaction.

There are a number of types of conflict to be found in games. If we look at the eight types of fun developed by Marc LeBlanc, conflict relates directly to challenge and indirectly to narrative and expression, and I would argue that fantasy, fellowship, and discovery benefit from the existence of conflict.[1] Challenge is the enjoyment we get by striving with and overcoming obstacles. To be mechanically conflict-free, a game would need to lack challenge. Expression is the enjoyment we get from creating or expressing ourselves. The primary conflict found in expression is inner conflict. My inhibitions, skill level, and imagination provide limits and obstacles to my ability to express myself. My argument for fantasy, fellowship, and discovery is that overcoming obstacles or challenges adds a sense of purpose and drama to our make believe, our social interactions, and our exploration. And lastly, there is narrative conflict which is already a topic of study within literary criticism.

Narrative conflict in literature, loosely defined as a person (or character) vs. the source of the conflict, has long been divided into a half-dozen types: character vs. self, character vs. character, character vs. nature, character vs. supernatural/fate/god, character vs. technology, and character vs. society. The existence of narrative conflict provides characters with the impetus for action and gives meaning to the action. A story without a conflict is a story without a plot.[2] In board games, conflict-free themes can seem at odds with the win condition, can seem pasted-on, or can seem half-baked where the players don't fully know why they are taking the actions of the game.[3] A cutthroat game of flower growing can make sense if players are given thematic context for why the mechanics are cutthroat. But if the theme is anodyne and the gameplay is "take that," players will feel the mismatch of conflict-free theme and conflict-filled mechanisms.

In video games, we find another way to designate conflict: player vs. player (PvP), player vs. the environment (PvE), and various combinations of the two.[4] These terms let players know who is the antagonist, in other words who is trying to kill you—the game or other players or both. Board games use similar terms—one vs. all, semi-coop, traitor mechanism, etc.—in order to specify who the antagonist of the players is. However, the consistency and similarity of the video game terms to narrative conflict terms is useful when attempting to examine the types of conflict found in board games.

By comparing how conflict is described in literature and video games to how conflict exists in board games, I have created some general terms for the main modes of conflict. There are three main types of player conflict in board games:

- *Player vs. Self:* This could be expressed by players trying to beat their high score or best time or by players accessing their creativity or self-expression. This conflict is most prominent in party games and some solo games, but also exists in games where there are avenues for creative expression within the components and rules, such as engine builders. There is often tension between a player's creativity and optimal scoring, which may or may not be a desirable trait in a particular game.
- *Player vs. Game:* This is the challenge the game poses to the player. Almost all games have this conflict to an extent (and to the extent that what we consider a game is something with rules that restrict our freedom of choice). But we see this conflict most prominently in solo games, cooperative games, and multi-player solitaire games. A subset of this conflict is *player vs. time*, where the game imposes time constraints on the players.
- *Player vs. Player:* This exists whenever a subset of players can defeat other players. This conflict is magnified by direct player interaction, especially negative player interaction.[5]

So far, we have seen that several types of fun generate or benefit from conflict and that types or styles of gameplay can provide different types of conflict. Now let's look at an important intersection of theme and game structure: the win condition. Specifically in this case, what or why are we trying to win? Some games, even thematic games, don't provide a reason for why you want to win. However, most games have at least one of the following three goals:

- *Beat your opponent(s) in a competition:* If there are victory points in a game, it is likely a competition. Races are also competitions. Earning the most money is a competition. Does the game measure your performance against other players? It's a competition. To double down on the theme, many games explicitly state that player characters (or avatars) are thematically challenged to a competition with their peers. Competitions can be PvP, team-based, or against a game AI.
- *Destroy or eliminate your opponent(s)*: Most games with player elimination, or that end when one player is knocked out, have this type of victory condition. However, you could be destroying non-player characters (NPCs) controlled by a game AI (and vice versa). In team-based games, one team may win when all, or a majority, of members of the opposing team are eliminated, such as in the social deduction, covert-conflict party game, *Werewolf*.
- *Outlast your opponent(s)*: This is the rarest goal to find on its own. Usually, it is combined with one of the other two. Here, you are not actively fighting other players. Instead, the focus is on surviving what the game throws at you. The goal is to continue to be able to play after other players have failed. In *Get Bit!* players are swimming away from a shark. The player in last place in a round will lose a limb. Players who have lost four limbs are eliminated. The player in front when only two players are left wins. Dance marathons from the first half of the twentieth century fall into this category, as do traditional card games such as Slap Jack, where the goal is to be the player with all the cards.

In order to have a well-knitted theme, your thematic goals should align with whether your game is a competition, an elimination game, and/or a survival game.

Now let's return to the question of what a completely conflict-free game would look like. I posit that a conflict-free game would have no win condition. The prospect of winning, and especially losing, generates conflict. Likewise, challenge generates conflict; so conflict-free games cannot be challenging to the extent that it cannot present difficult or meaningful decisions. Self-expression can generate internal challenge and thus conflict. Narrative is largely defined by the conflict of obstacles that get between a character and their goals. Yes, I am saying that a conflict-free game can't have traditional storytelling or much in the way of creativity. What kind of game are we left with?

RPGs provide some interesting options if all you want is a game without competition or a win condition. However, due to their narrative nature, RPGs contain a form of conflict.[6] For conflict-free games, I think we have to look at video games. The types of fun least associated with conflict are sensation and submission. A game that delights the senses (honestly, that's optional) and functions as a rote pastime with goals and rules but no obstacles other than the time commitment to playing is a game that is truly conflict-free. Video games that focus primarily on "grinding" or "farming" stand out as exemplars of submission-focused games. Other games that fit this category are *Candyland* and bingo, because they lack challenge, expression, and narrative, even though they have win conditions. Indeed, bingo is an example of a submission-focused game that also has a high degree of fellowship.

I have seen many discussions from designers looking to create conflict-free games. Most of those designers would find my definition of conflict-free games to be boring. This is where we find a mismatch of definitions. When people talk about conflict, they may be referring to violence, domination, artificial scarcity promoting needless competition, an us vs. them mentality, antagonism, or just an unhealthy obsession with winning. Games can be free of all of these things but still have conflict. The conflict found in an educational game may be around the obstacles of learning the concepts rather than winning. Overcoming obstacles is often a learning process, and learning usually involves overcoming obstacles. Also, as we have seen, the conflict in a game does not have to come from pitting players against each other. By understanding what conflict is, we are better able to carefully craft the sorts of conflict found in our games, both thematically and mechanically.

But what does player conflict have to do with theme-building? Conflict is plot, and if we are to knit our theme to our mechanics, we must first understand how conflict works in our games. Thematic conflict should mirror mechanical conflict. Player goals should mirror character goals. Game structure and story structure should resemble each other.[7] The rest of this chapter will discuss ways of expressing plot in your game structurally.

CONVERTING GOALS TO ACTIONS

In Chapter 2, we looked at types of actions from the perspective of how they express theme on a per action-unit basis. Chapter 5 will look at how goals and obstacles fit together to tell a story. Before we get there, we must make another mechanical detour. The previous section discussed how goals and obstacles generate conflict. This section covers how actions can be used to mechanically express the goals and obstacles of the theme.

Actions are governed by rules. Anything that occurs outside of the rules is not an action but rather meta-play. Actions are usually organized into turns, rounds, and/or phases. Turns are not synonymous with actions. Examples of actions are "move up to two spaces," "attack," "collect resources," etc., while a turn may contain multiple actions. Actions can be divided into multiple categories based on the goal of the action. Actions can combine multiple of the action categories discussed below, such as deploying a unit while generating a value for it. By having a clear understanding of the mechanical goal of an action, we can better align that goal with a thematic goal. I divide mechanical actions into eight categories.

- *Acquisition.* Actions that result in a game's elements being claimed exclusively by a single player are acquisition actions. Acquired elements may be either secret information from all players, private information known only to the acquiring player, or shared information. Mechanical example: drawing cards face-up or face-down. If my thematic goal is to acquire something, I will need an acquisition mechanic.
- *Deployment.* Actions that move game elements from a hidden or inactive status to a visible, active status are deployment actions. Deployed elements may be played onto a personal play-space or a shared play-space. Mechanical example: playing cards into a tableau. Deployment actions fulfill goals of exploration, claiming territory, troop mustering, combat, resource gathering, etc.
- *Spatial Adjustment.* Actions that change the physical location of already deployed game elements are spatial adjustment actions. Physical location includes height, such as components in a stack. Adjusted pieces may belong to the player taking the action, another player, or be a part of the shared play-state. Mechanical example:

moving tokens around a track. Spatial adjustment fulfills goals of troop advancement, racing, and all of the deployment goals listed above.

- *Value Adjustment.* Actions that change the assigned value of a game element are value adjustment actions. Value adjustments are most often numeric. Value adjustments can occur to a player's elements, their opponent's elements, or shared elements. Adjustments to a player's elements tend to increase value, while adjustments to opponents' elements tend to decrease value. Value adjustments are commonly used to mitigate luck. Mechanical example: attack damage. Value adjustments fulfill goals of combat resolution, market fluctuation, auctions, negotiations, growth (such as plants or animals), location or item improvements/developments, etc.
- *Value Generation.* Actions that set the value of game elements that were previously null are value generation actions. Value generation is most commonly luck-based, with the frequent use of dice to determine a value. This category is largely a subset of value adjustment. Mechanical example: dealing cards randomly to auction board spaces that have set values. Value generation fulfills many of the same goals as value adjustment but sometimes places control of how the values are assigned or what the values are in the hands of the players, like in the case of *QE*, an auction game where players can bid any amount no matter how absurd.
- *Social Leveraging.* Actions that change the perceived value of game elements are social leveraging actions. Changes in perceived value do not change the assigned value of the game element. This category is the subjective version of value adjustment. Social leveraging nearly always includes discussing the play-state with other players, with the goal of getting other players to act the way you want them to. In order to fall into the social leveraging action category, the actions must be a part of the game as described in the rules. Mechanical examples: negotiating, bluffing/lying, alliances. Social Leveraging fulfills goals of amassing political power, garnering votes for an agenda, getting the best deal on a resource, hiding your identity, etc. This concept is addressed further in Chapter 6, in the section about player strategies.

- *Element Generation.* Actions that create game elements as a part of gameplay are element generation actions. Element generation actions are most common in party games. Mechanical examples: drawing, acting/miming, giving clues, and storytelling. Element generation can fulfill goals of development planning, map exploration, and route building in addition to storytelling.
- *Null Actions.* Actions that leave the play-space unchanged are null actions. The most common example is the option to pass on a player's turn.

What about failure? Not all actions succeed. Actions do not have to succeed to qualify for their category. Attempting an acquisition action and failing still qualifies the action as an acquisition action. In fact, many mechanisms are built around the high potential for failure. Auction and dexterity games have high levels of acquisition failure for highly desired pieces and lower levels of failure for less desired pieces. All social leveraging actions have a high expected failure rate, as those actions rely on the subjective ability to persuade other players. Spatial adjustment has a middling failure rate. Players can be out-maneuvered and blocked from moving into a space, but will stop having fun if this happens too often. Deployment has a low failure rate, because not being able to activate pieces is not fun and slows game tempo. Value adjustment and value generation also have low failure rates due to frustration factors. Instead, players are usually offered mitigation and retaliation options rather than the ability to cancel a player's turn. Element generation, by its nature, has zero failure rate. Provided all players are participating, no matter what quality of element they create, the elements created will be used in play. Whether or not those elements are effective generally falls into other categories.

Using Action Categories

One way to use these categories is simply as a way of diagnosing mechanical issues in gameplay. When a design needs a mechanism, or needs a replacement mechanism, I look at what the goal of the mechanism should be, then examine the various mechanisms that best reach that goal while fitting the constraints of the overall game: "This way of acquiring cards doesn't work. What is another *acquisition* action I can put here instead?" Many actions are blends of the categories. For example, dice combat includes value generation via dice and value adjustment to a player's damage track. Combining multiple categories in an action or breaking them into separate actions requires understanding the purposes the actions fulfill in the game.

More relevant to this book, these categories can be used when designing a game theme-first. As stated, action categories look at the goals of an action. Thematic narrative is made up of goals and obstacles. When we break down the goals within the theme, we can start applying action categories (and then mechanisms) to those goals. Usually, goals involve what characters want. If that want is a physical object, acquisition actions may be used to obtain the object. By understanding that a goal is acquisition, I can evaluate mechanisms—existing mechanisms and those I invent—by how well they meet the goal of the theme.

The types of actions used in gameplay and their failure rate will provide the choices, tension, and challenges of the game. In other words, the obstacles. Games would not be interesting if players were gifted with everything they needed to succeed. The same is true for stories. What is it that prevents characters from achieving their goals? Weighty decisions or difficult challenges in the mechanics should be reflected thematically. Lighter themes will ratchet down tension in a game and darker themes will increase tension. Obstacles that result in thematic consequences increase player investment in the story of the game.[8]

GAME WORLD VS. GAME STATE

The rest of this chapter looks at the areas of gameplay where theming is more important or less important. There is a core disambiguation you have to make when trying to integrate your mechanics with your theme: that of the game state and the game world. To understand the difference, we should first look at Gil Hova's "Player in Three Persons" model.[9] The model proposes three representatives of self in a game: the player, the avatar, and the agent. The player is the person playing the game; the avatar is the thematic representation of the player in the game; the agent is the mechanical representation of the player in the game.[10] Hova asserts that high overlap between agent and avatar results in a deeply thematic experience. I agree with him with one caveat: sometimes actions must be mechanical for simplicity's sake, so full overlap is rare.

Using Hova's model, we can broaden his lens to examine why sometimes theme and mechanisms don't mesh well. Game state refers to the mechanical progression of gameplay and thus interacts with the player through the agent. The game world interacts with the player through the avatar. When an element will affect the game world, it should be thematic. When an element only interacts with the agential side of play, trying to force a theme can feel unnatural. Let's look at some common mechanisms that seem to reject theming. In card-drafting games, the drafting phase is typically agential and separated from the theme. In order to make a drafting phase feel thematic, a game would have to relate the physical actions and mental decisions of selecting cards to the theme in a simulative way to overcome the strong agential decisions being made. Cards, especially in the hand, are inherently abstracted from the game world, with each thematic card essentially floating in space. This makes theming card acquisition difficult to do. The best example of thematic drafting is *Sushi Roll*, a dice-drafting game where the dice slide around on conveyor belt tiles. The action of selecting something chunky and placing it in front of you is the same action you take at an actual sushi restaurant. *Sushi Go!*, a card-drafting game, cannot express the same level of theme because passing a hand of cards doesn't feel similar enough to a conveyor belt sliding by. The mechanics of *Sushi Go!* are inspired by the theme, but the theme does not feel as present. Deck building games have the same problems and for the same reasons: the actions of acquiring and shuffling cards are too abstract (or too tied to our sense memory of playing abstract card games) to feel thematic.

These mechanisms primarily affect the game state and have little effect on the game world. If you take into account a player's emotional state throughout gameplay, you can turn agential play back into avatar play,[11] but often you are better off letting purely agential mechanisms remain somewhat abstract. You should still use thematic icons and art for visual consistency, but there is danger in pushing the theme too hard. Audiences want to watch movies that make them feel sad, not movies that claim to be sad without earning any real emotional payoff. Games that try too hard to be thematic—in the wrong ways—will feel weaker than games that understand where the emotional payoff of the theme comes from. Usually, in a multi-board game, you will have a board where the characters interact with locations and a board (or section of a board) that exists purely to track game state. *The Quacks of Quedlinburg* is an excellent example of this. The score board tracks the rounds and players' scores (and rat tails and ingredient unlocks). It is purely agential. The art is there, but players interact with it as players, not as alchemists. The player boards (and the ingredient market) exist in the game world. Players are placing ingredients in a pot hoping it will not explode. The theme is not overall simulative or transportive,[12] but it is still present and actions in the game world affect the narrative of the alchemists in the game world, however thin that narrative may be.

Thematic Upgrades

One place in particular that seems to trip up designers navigating the game state and game world is upgrades. Many euro games have upgrade boards or action selection boards that mix agential play with avatar play. The act of selecting from a menu of mechanical choices is usually abstract, but the choices are often thematic or a mix of thematic and abstract. Often, designers will design thematic core loops but seem to forget about the other sections of their games. Upgrade boards are merely one place where I see this the most.

Haspelknecht is a surprisingly thematic euro game about the early days of coal mining. The core loop of gameplay is compelling both narratively and gameplay-wise. However, the upgrade system is a thematic mess. The upgrade system in *Haspelknecht* provides much of the player interaction and takes up the majority of the shared play space. The upgrades have illustrations that point to the theme. Some of the mechanics are more thematic than others, but it's clear an effort at theming was made. I do not think the attempts at theming the upgrades are effective. Most of the time, you are giving up opportunities to interact with the (very fun) core loop in order to be rewarded by getting a weak, barely thematic upgrade. Astute players will realize that the mere act of having been to an upgrade spot is the most powerful way to get points in the game. The game is rewarding you for interacting with the much less fun part of the game by providing unthematic incentives. Do you want to mine all the coal? You will probably lose to the person going after the highest numeric value upgrade spots. One lesson here is that when you design a system that has players chasing purely numeric rewards, your theme will suffer.

Not every element of a game has to be thematic. I like the action apportionment mechanics in *Haspelknecht* and they are very abstract. But those mechanics apply to what I can do as a player. The player board is purely thematic and applies to what the characters are doing. The upgrade system applies to my mine, my resources, my characters, but also my action economy. It isn't one thing or the other. I want it to be thematic because I enjoy theme. However, I like the purely abstract action selection mechanism, because its system applies to me as a player (in addition to being fun); so perhaps, if the upgrade system were more abstract, I could like it more for its consistency if nothing else.

Later chapters will dwell more on the importance of win conditions and player powers needing to be thematic. *Haspelknecht* is another example of gameplay goals needing to line up with thematic goals. I wanted to mine coal, pump water, and expand shafts. The game wanted me to race for special action opportunities that were more expensive than the regular actions without being particularly better, but the act of choosing them would earn me end game points. What I am looking for is thematic incentives to interact with what the designer intends to be a central draw of the game. As a player, my goal for each turn is to (1) do the fun thing and (2) make progress toward winning. As a player who likes theme and is playing a thematic game, "do the fun thing" means taking a thematic action that impacts the game world and not just the game state. When I mine coal, that coal is removed and a new coal vein is exposed. When I take an upgrade, I have access to other future upgrades on the board. One of those two options is significantly more fun than the other because of the way it interacts with my imagination.

Some games get a lot of mileage out of putting "do the fun thing" in tension with "make progress toward winning." But often those games present that tension in choices you are making within a single system, such as engine building. You can build your engine creatively or efficiently, and one way will give you a sense of satisfaction and the other will give you the victory. You can play efficiently within thematic systems. You will have a harder time playing thematically within unthematic systems. Ideally, each upgrade should function as a mini-achievement or short-term goal that is just as thematic as the overall goal of gameplay.

In general, changes to the game world, like upgrades, need to feel thematic and motivated by the world. If they are important to good strategy, they should also be incentivized by scoring and rewards. Upgrades give players an opportunity to make improvements to the game world. This is both psychologically and narratively appealing. I would recommend trying to keep all the actions offered on such a menu at the same level of thematic expression. Flipping back and forth between thematic and abstract choices feels messy and confusing as a player.

Strong thematic choices in elements that affect the game world are always a good idea. However, the trickiest pieces of thematic design are the elements that aren't clearly in the game world or outside of it. Additionally, pushing too much theme into primarily agential elements can be a mistake. Knowing where to focus on theme and where not to is an important skill for a designer to have. Knowing which parts of your game affect the game world and which only affect the game state leads to better thematic design.

UTILIZING PAUSES

By identifying which elements of your game take place outside of the game world, you can also take steps to minimize the breaks in immersion.[13] Anyone who has taken an acting class should be able to tell you that audiences don't find actors pausing for laughter to be unrealistic. For an audience member, laughing effectively stopped their perception of time. We can achieve something similar in board games. An entire agential phase can occur without disrupting immersion if players experience the phase as a pause and not an interruption. Interruptions are jarring and unwelcome breaks in the flow of the game. Pauses can be used for pacing, to catch your breath, or to whet your imagination. Setting up a new scenario in a campaign, for instance, can prime players for the action that is to come by teasing the sorts of obstacles they might encounter, such as the terrain. Action selection menus can function the same way in a euro game, teasing options for how the game world can develop based on the choices made by the agent. Learning how to pause rather than interrupt the flow of play creates integrated experiences that will feel more thematic even when they technically aren't, they're just better executed agentially.

Pauses are moments in gameplay when the game state takes precedence over the game world or when busywork intrudes upon the rhythm of play. Pauses allow players to catch their breath and check in on the game state. Pauses provide structure in the form of guideposts throughout the game. Pauses occur at the beginning and end of rounds, at the end of turns, during scoring, etc.

Handled poorly, pauses can become interruptions. People have the ability to sustain a state of mind even when something distracts them. Imagine, for example, waking up in the night and needing a glass of water. If you are like me, you will leave the lights off and keep your task as brief as possible so as to never become fully alert, which makes returning to sleep that much easier. However, turning the lights on and having a conversation with the cat[14] can make returning to sleep much more difficult.

Pauses occur during transitions. The designer's job is to smooth transitions as much as possible. Carefully designed transitions will provide the benefits of a pause without breaking the absorption of the players. Good graphic design is a requirement. Intuitive rules are important. Transitions that make sense thematically also help.

If more time is spent in tinkering with the game state rather than the game world, pauses will inevitably become interruptions. This applies to setup, take-down, scoring, rules referencing, some AI management, etc., but also applies to other pure game state mechanics *if* the appeal of the game is interacting with the game world. Usually, the draw of a drafting game is mechanical appeal just as much as (or more than) thematic appeal. However, the hook of an adventure game is getting to interact with the game world. Thus, the adventure game is less tolerant of purely game state mechanisms than the drafting game is. This becomes an issue because adventure games (and narrative-rich games more generally) are usually more complicated than drafting games, and complicated games tend to have more upkeep. So we find ourselves with the issue that the games that are most harmed by interruptions tend to be games more susceptible to them. War games have solved this issue by making the simulative rules and upkeep a feature not a bug, but that has limited the audience for those games considerably.

Here are some guidelines for handling pauses:

- *Minimize busywork.* Busywork, or upkeep, is always a pause and often an interruption.
- *Plan pauses that minimize downtime.* Maybe your round structure allows for partial simultaneous play and partial turn-based. Pauses and distinct phases go hand in hand and provide non-mechanical benefits to the experience of play. The rulebook could also suggest that players who finish their turns or upkeep first should begin to set up for the next round.
- *Theme everything, at first.* Go overboard on thematic justification then pull back based on what playtesters find to be too much. You may find new ways to bring parts of the game state into your game world.[15]

- *Theme around the action of the game.* If your game world is simply layered onto your game state, you may not have any problems because the game state never will interrupt the game world, because the game world will not feel present during gameplay. If, however, your game world is present in part of the game but not the rest, you are likely to inadvertently design interruptions into your game. Theming the game more closely around the gameplay is the more fun solution to this problem.

Remember that pauses are not bad and provide necessary structure to a game. The designer's job is to intentionally design pauses that augment rather than detract from the player experience. Plan pauses so they don't become interruptions. Understanding pauses and interruptions leads to better experience design.

Exercise 4.1: Pick one of your designs or a published game. What types of conflict are present? What goals are present? Do the mechanical obstacles align with the thematic obstacles?

Exercise 4.2: Pick a light to medium weight published game. List all the action categories used in the game. Do the goals of the actions line up with the goals in the theme?

Exercise 4.3: Pick a published thematic game. List the elements that exist in the game world and those that exist outside of it. Do those elements exist in harmony? What could the designer(s) have done thematically to improve the gameplay experience?

Exercise 4.4: Pick a published game and identify all of the pauses that occur during gameplay. Do any of these pauses become interruptions? What could the designer(s) have done to improve the pauses?

NOTES

1. Marc LeBlanc developed the eight types of fun, which are frequently used in discussions of how players derive enjoyment in different ways when playing games. The eight types are sensation, fantasy, narrative, challenge, fellowship, discovery, expression, and submission (Hunicke, LeBlanc, and Zubek, "MDA: A Formal Approach to Game Design and Game Research": 3.)
2. I am admittedly coming from a western point of view. There are other ways to think about narrative. However, I think that for most designers, adding conflict to the theme/narrative will help with integration as most games also contain conflict in the form of obstacles to winning.
3. This is assuming that the game contains challenges, but the theme attempts to be conflict-free.

4. Specifically, PvPvE and PvEvP. These terms are relegated to only a few specific types of video games, but I am assured by enthusiasts that they refer to two different play styles.
5. The book *Rules of Play* delves into the many different ways players can play in opposition to other players (Katie Salen and Eric Zimmerman, *Rules of Play: Game Design Fundamentals*. Cambridge, MA: The MIT Press, 2004: 250.) For the purpose of discussing where conflict originates from, a detailed discussion here seems unnecessary. Negative player strategies are discussed in Chapter 6.
6. The keepsake solo RPG genre contains some attempts at narrative free RPG-like game-like objects, but these are openly pushing the boundaries on what can be considered a game, so I have left them out of this discussion. I have likewise left out walking simulators and other video games that stretch the definition of game.
7. Game structures are discussed in Chapter 3 and narrative structure is discussed in Chapter 5.
8. This idea is explored more in the Chapter 5 discussion of thematic story structure.
9. Gil Hova, "The Well-Integrated Theme: How to Get Theme and Mechanism to Work Together in Your Game," YouTube video, posted by "Double Exposure, Inc." June 2, 2021. https://www.youtube.com/watch?v=-kjDsNt5DiA&list=WL&index=78.
10. Throughout the rest of the book, I will refer to player characters as avatars and use the term characters to apply to both player characters and non-player characters alike.
11. This is discussed more in Chapter 11 in the section on improving thematic engagement.
12. Placing ingredients in a swirling cauldron approaches a simulative action, but the implementation is more metaphoric.
13. Here, immersion can mean either transportation or absorption.
14. Usually a one-sided conversation, although some cats are more vocal than others.
15. The counterpoint to this is found in Chapter 12, in the section When to Dial Back Theme.

REFERENCES

1. Hunicke, Robin, Marc LeBlanc, and Robert Zubek. "MDA: A Formal Approach to Game Design and Game Research." AAAI Workshop - Technical Report 1, 2004: 3.
2. Salen, Katie and Eric Zimmerman. *Rules of Play: Game Design Fundamentals*. Cambridge, MA: The MIT Press, 2004.
3. Hova, Gil. "The Well-Integrated Theme: How to Get Theme and Mechanism to Work Together in Your Game." YouTube video. Posted by "Double Exposure, Inc," June 2, 2021. https://www.youtube.com/watch?v=-kjDsNt5DiA&list=WL&index=78.

GAMES REFERENCED

Werewolf
Get Bit!
Slap Jack
Candyland
Bingo
QE
Sushi Roll
Sushi Go!
The Quacks of Quedlinburg
Haspelknecht

CHAPTER 5

Narrative Structure

NARRATIVE-BASED GAMES ARE TYPES of board games that contain specific story-based thematic elements and (usually) chunks of narrative text, which are supposed to be read before or after indicated sections of gameplay. Typically, these games have specified start and end scenarios, but will often let player choice dictate the order of the middle scenarios. This style of game attempts to model traditional narrative structure while also preserving player agency. Storytelling games, by contrast, are games where players improvisationally construct stories based on prompts provided by the game. Both genres place a strong emphasis on traditional styles of narrative.

Non-narrative games do not make use of narrative text or traditional story structure during gameplay. Non-narrative board games can still have narratives. Talking about narrative within non-narrative games seems paradoxical, but a game's narrative is the story of what occurs in a game. Narratives in non-narrative board games are structured in ways other than traditional narratives. One of the ways we talk about narrative in games is the emergent narrative, one that evolves out of play instead of being written before-hand. Many games appear to present slice-of-life style narratives,[1] such as agricultural-themed games. We limit our designs when we believe that narrative has to look a certain way and that everything else outside of traditional narrative just functions as window-dressing. This chapter discusses narrative techniques which can be applied to any style of thematic game to create a stronger narrative. Throughout this chapter, the term narrative is used to mean the types of stories that occur during gameplay, rather than in reference to traditional narrative structures.

DOI: 10.1201/9781003453765-7

NARRATIVE FRAMING

Within theme-building we encounter narrative framing. Narrative framing is the boundaries of the story and how the story is expressed. Think of narrative framing as similar to cinematography. In film, you can have a good script, good acting, and good directing, but if the cinematographer does a bad job, your movie might be incomprehensible. Similarly, in board games, you can have a good story in the rulebook that describes your world and you can have good mechanics, but if the theme is not knitted to the mechanics, the game won't make narrative sense. Narrative framing is a tool we can use to help us knit together our theme and mechanics.

Narrative framing focuses on who gets the spotlight and which parts of the story get told. Board games by their nature have to present an abstraction of a story. Narrative framing is the process of deciding which details get airbrushed out and which details get emphasized. There are a few basic questions to ask to determine your narrative framing.

- *Who are the players*? You may have a story in mind, but the type of game you are trying to make, the structure and primary mechanisms, will partially determine who the main characters should be. In cooperative games, characters have a single purpose and work together to achieve it. In competitive games, characters have conflicting desires even if they have the same goal. In a competitive game, you generally do not want to depict characters who are all on the same team thematically unless you include an element of betrayal. Players could control separate teams of characters, however. Your choice of who the avatars are has a strong effect on how players will relate to your game world. Characters are the way that players access the world of the game. Sometimes changing who the main characters are in the story will focus the story on the type of experience you want players to have.
- *What are the characters doing*? *What are their goals*? A character's goals should line up with the overall win condition and/or their personal win condition. Tying characters' goals to the win condition is an effective way to make a game feel significantly more thematic. Even if the mechanics do not change, changing goals thematically can raise the emotional stakes which in turn increases player investment in the game narrative. Do players care about the main task of

the theme? That goal should feel important enough to the avatars that the players become invested in achieving it.

- *What actions are the characters taking? How are they progressing toward their goals?* The actions of a game should be the method by which a character achieves their goal. Actions should feel "in character" for avatars and non-player characters alike. If a character acts in a way that doesn't flow from the logic of the narrative, players will disconnect from the story. Actions are how the story is told, so retheme actions as necessary to produce the best experience.
- *Why are the characters trying to achieve a certain goal? Why are they using certain methods?* Goals and the methods used to achieve them should make narrative sense. It should be clear why the characters want what they want and why they employ the methods that they use. Either through the types of actions available to a character, their unique powers, or flavor text, let players know what the character values. A character's values give insight into why the character is trying to achieve a certain goal. Avatars are discussed in more depth in Chapters 6 and 7.
- *When and where is the theme happening?* Setting is very important for providing context clues to players about the game world. Players can use their existing knowledge of a genre, time period, or location to fill in some of the gaps in the theme. This means that your chosen setting can also provide an experience you don't want players to have. For example, *Puerto Rico*'s setting combined with brown-colored worker discs suggests that the players are slave owners, even if the game makes an effort to deny that fact by labeling the discs "colonists." The rethemed version, *Puerto Rico 1897*, shifted the setting to be post-slavery. Changing the setting to occur after slavery was abolished is much more effective theming than simply trying to label the workers something unoffensive. Setting is discussed more in Chapter 8.

When playtesting, pay attention to how players react to your theme. Playtesters, especially those who are veterans in the hobby, are quick to give feedback about mechanics but not narrative. You may have to ask what they thought of the story of the game. I would recommend giving a two sentence explanation of the game world prior to playing the game, then ask if their experiences mesh with your vision of what the story is. As a designer, you likely see all the background worldbuilding that may not be apparent to the average player. A short narrative introduction to the game world helps establish your narrative framing which you and your players can use as a standard to measure the game's experience by.

When you design, try to feel invested in your characters' goals. "Why should I care?" is the question I ask most often in the early design process, before mechanical things like balance come into play. I include this question here, because I find that the solution to lack of investment is usually found in narrative framing. Players should care not only about winning but that their character reaches their goals. If I change the perspective or emphasis of my narrative to something more compelling, player excitement about my game will increase even if the mechanics stay the same. Player investment in their character's success is an indication that the narrative is compelling.

Before I move on, I want to include what I consider to be a poor example of narrative framing. *Love Letter* makes no thematic sense. Mechanically, players are trying primarily to eliminate other players, which does not line up with the theme of delivering letters at all. There is no sense of "delivering something" in the mechanics. The princess shouldn't be able to carry letters to herself. Instead of having letters that must be delivered, players *receive* "tokens of affection." There are a number of ways this game could be reframed to knit the theme to the mechanics.[2] The setting of a masquerade could fit with the mechanism of secret roles. Spies infiltrating a castle might work as a theme. Here's one more extreme attempt to reframe the theme (without changing the art, components, or mechanics): the princess is planning a coup. She must get messages out to various supporters. The player who gets more of her messages out of the castle will become her chief advisor. Or another less extreme possibility is that the player who can best navigate cutthroat court politics will receive the princess's hand in marriage as measured by the tokens of affection they receive from her. That one sticks the closest to the current theme but disposes of the "delivering letters" aspect. It also accounts for the player elimination and the competitive nature of the game world. If you reframe the tokens of affection to love notes, you might not even need to change the name of the game (maybe make it Love Letters).

The point here is not that *Love Letter* is a bad game. *Love Letter* is an excellent game. The point is that often what makes a game thematically knitted has more to do with narrative framing than it does with mechanical design. Reframing a theme can create greater narrative investment in a game by increasing the thematic logic of the mechanics. Increasing thematic logic makes rules easier to learn and remember. It also strengthens the thematic hook, because players don't have to rely on your description of the theme but can describe the game using their own thematic language when they have a strong investment in the theme. Finding themes or thematic elements that better frame mechanics allows designers to better signal what kind of game experience is to be had through play.

Scope and Resolution

Two important concepts within narrative framing are scope and resolution. Scope refers to how focused or wide-ranging the theme is. Scope is largely a function of setting.[3] The types of actions in wide-scope civilization building games and narrow-scope civilization building games are going to be similar, largely because the civilization genre dictates that they must be. It is the thematic details of the setting that establish the scope. While both wide- and narrow-scope civilization games will have buildings and tech advancement and leaders, a wide-scope game will cover all of world history, such as in *Through the Ages: a New Story of Civilization*, where a narrow-scope game may only cover the bronze age in central Eurasia, like in *Antike II*.

Resolution refers to how detailed or abstracted the theme is.[4] A low resolution game abstracts most of the theme. A high resolution game models the theme as much as possible with the mechanics.[5] Low resolution games may or may not have complex mechanics, but a high resolution game must have at least a minimum amount of complexity in order to accurately model the theme. The wider the scope, the more complexity is needed for a high resolution game. Long war-games tend to be wide scope and high resolution. Civilization games are usually wide scope and low resolution. Euro games are often low resolution regardless of scope.

Increasing resolution adds complexity, because mechanics have to be added to model the theme. The wider the scope, the more complexity required for high resolution.[6] Greater complexity means not only more rules overhead but usually longer gameplay time. Narrow-scope themes can achieve high resolution without as much added complexity. High resolution also requires greater levels of research when developing nonfiction themes. The wider the scope, the more research is required.

High resolution, regardless of scope, results in more work for designers. Many popular themed games are referred to as "essentially abstracts," which is to say that they are low resolution games. Why, therefore, should designers strive for higher resolutions in their themes?

- *Players like thematic games.* They like abstracted games, too, but we already have those in abundance. Higher resolution themes, especially in shorter, more accessible games, can more easily stand out from the crowd of games published each year.
- *Higher resolution themes have better hooks and are easier to market.* Trading in the ancient world is a very generic and overdone theme. *Passing through Petra* is a higher resolution version of that theme that is more memorable because of its specificity. The game uses the geography of Petra to shape what resources, in this case merchants, are available to players.
- *Higher resolution themes have more intuitive rules.* Again, low resolution mechanics are more abstract. Abstract rules are less intuitive than rules with thematic logic behind them.

I want to see more high resolution, narrow-scope games. I love deep, thematic detail in game mechanisms, and I think that is much easier to achieve in a narrow-scope theme. However, simply adding scope and resolution to your toolkit allows you to adjust the dials of your theme to better achieve your design vision or better connect with your intended audience.

To conclude this section, frame the narrative to fit the events of gameplay. Do so in a way that makes the mechanics and the emergent story make sense. Use scope and resolution to dial in your theme to achieve your intended play experience. Better narrative framing allows players to become invested in a game by way of the narrative. Invested players become the core audience of any game.

THEMATIC STORY STRUCTURE

Rules can act as a cinematographer, framing the experience, building and releasing tension, and providing a structure for the story of the game. Rules can also be expediters, providing quick checkpoints and then getting out of the way of a narrative. Most thematic games have some of both. Knowing what your rules convey and what they *can* convey helps you guide your design to a more thematic experience. The rest of this chapter will look at some specific ways rules can inform narrative.

Gameplay narrative could be a book by itself. Narrative structure is a complex subject in more traditional storytelling mediums to begin with. On top of that, mechanical game arcs are a layered topic for which there is no single, authoritative reference source.[7] And discussing narrative arcs in games requires knowledge of both. I will leave the subject of game arcs as much as possible to other people[8] and try to focus on some general concepts around narrative structure in board games.

Narrative structure in games is a more detailed view of a game's story than narrative framing. Narrative framing looks broadly at how the narrative is positioned to the overall action of the game. Narrative structure looks at how the story progresses, action by action or goal by goal. The concern of this section and my proposed model is that a game's emergent narrative makes sense and provides a satisfying experience. Once you are comfortable crafting games with a basic narrative structure, you can experiment with game arcs, pauses, progressive goals (discussed in the following section), and so on to build rich, compelling game narratives.

I have seen board gameplay described as "all rising action." I disagree, although I allow that that is a simple way to align most gameplay with traditional three-act narrative structure. Any game with a single, mechanical pivot point, like *Clank!*, has both rising and falling action. A boss-battler could be considered a single, climactic scene. *Small World*, an area majority, open conflict game, leans heavily into falling action as factions go into decline. Traditional narrative structures are easiest to incorporate into games when a game has a campaign mode or sequential scenarios, because of the ability to include different challenges and challenge levels that lead to a sense of story progression over multiple gaming sessions.

There are, of course, different types of narrative structure, from slice-of-life to five-act to absurdism. I'm not sure that translating gameplay arcs to existing, literary narrative structures is all that useful to designers. I propose an analysis style that comes from the study of acting: scene work. I won't describe how actors go about scene work here.[9] Instead, I will jump straight to my suggested mode of narrative analysis.

Scene work or scene analysis for game narrative starts with goals. The avatar should have one major goal that drives them to perform the actions

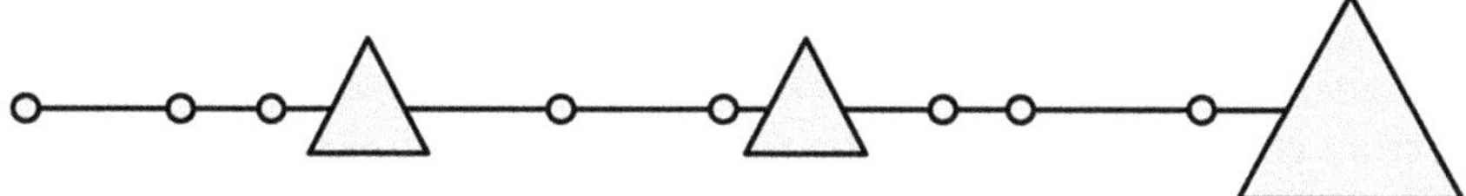

FIGURE 5.1 A model of three "scenes" in a game. The smaller triangles represent minor goals and the large triangle represents overall goals.

of the game. That goal should align with the win condition of the game. The avatar will have any number of minor goals. Those goals will align with actions taken or attempted in the game. Minor goals might include completing a set of objects or achieving an objective first or claiming a card before someone else can. If the minor goals tend to fall into stages during gameplay that shift from one stage to the next, then the game has distinct scenes. If not, the game may only have one scene. Individual scenes will have different goals and strategies, but will further the major goal of the game (Figure 5.1).[10]

Believable goals, especially minor goals, are the key to compelling characters. If I believe that a character is acting in accordance with their desires, that character comes alive. As a player, if character motivation makes sense, then I will be emotionally invested in my character. In a game without characters, I can still be invested in actions that further my goals thematically. However, I increasingly believe that it is interesting character motivations, not interesting plots, that matter for emotional investment.[11] Interesting stories will emerge if attention is paid to what characters want and what they are willing to do to get it.

Of course, scenes are not just made up of goals, but obstacles and actions and resolutions of conflict. All of which should be pushing the player toward the major goal. Within a scene, minor goals will have obstacles that must be overcome by actions. Those goals are resolved and replaced by the next set of goals, all of which are steps to achieve the major goal. Thinking in terms of goals and scenes can help ensure that the game narrative is thematically satisfying.

You may find it helpful to think in terms of three act structure. You may find your game narratives naturally want to shape themselves into traditional structure, because that style of storytelling feels familiar and satisfying. There is nothing wrong with that. But designers do not need to feel limited by traditional structures.[12]

Compounding Thematic Elements

Certain mechanics can help provide a narrative to your game by connecting goal to goal or by having game world elements interact thematically with the progression of the game state. If your design goal includes a transportive thematic experience—the feeling of being transported into a theme—a knitted theme may not be enough to provide that experience. You will need to go a step further by using elements that enhance the narrative structure of your game. In order to provide a deeper thematic experience, narrative elements must build on one another to add texture and tension to gameplay. There are a number of techniques you can employ that all fall under the umbrella of compounding thematic elements.

When thematic elements are presented as separate items that primarily interact mechanically but not thematically with each other, a game will provide a thematic experience that is nonetheless more strongly focused on the mechanical experience. When thematic elements build on each other and respond to each other, the resulting experience will have a stronger focus on theme.

Compounding thematic elements indicate a dynamic game world to players. A dynamic and responsive world provides a deeper thematic experience than a static world. Compounding elements may be as simple as synergies between resources, such as spending wood to turn raw food into cooked food. For more dramatic effects, you can utilize one or more of the following techniques.

Progressive goals are way points or win conditions that change as players progress through the game. Open world games and certain kinds of campaign games may employ progressive goals in order to hide the main conflict or antagonist from players at the beginning of the game. *Forgotten Waters* and other app-driven, adventure, narrative-heavy games can gradually provide story elements based on what the players have already done in the game. Other games may present all possible win conditions up front, but some may be locked until certain conditions are met. These types of goals must be tightly woven with the theme to produce a compounding thematic effect. So, while the "You Win" card in *Space Base*—a card that if purchased unlocks an alternate victory condition for that player—is a progressive goal, it is not a thematic goal and thus does not qualify as a compounding thematic element.

One way to keep players engaged with the theme is to have outside forces intrude on them during play. This can break players out of a pure numbers/efficiency mindset when executed well. Persistent effects, positive or negative, can shift player focus back to the game world. These effects are most impactful when layered on top of a thematic core game loop. Persistent effects can be either individual effects or global events that affect every player. Global events can be used to increase tension by providing an escalating threat to the players. Persistent effects can also raise tension by afflicting players with multiple negative effects at once. Multiple individual negative effects are a safer design choice for cooperative games, where a temporary goal may be to rescue a player from their negative effects. Multiple individual effects in competitive games will likely feel unfair to the player who falls behind as a result of the effects. Global events are particularly poignant in competitive games, because they can unite the players in moments of shared frustration or elation.

The goal of compounding thematic elements is to create a game world that feels dynamic and a game arc that has thematic tension. Designers are lauded for their ability to interweave mechanisms together. The same care can be taken to interweave theme so that the end result is a game that is both thematically and mechanically compelling. By focusing on mechanics that affect avatar goals, you can create a game world that feels both dynamic and more narratively compelling.

INCITING INCIDENTS

The following two sections look at methods of narrative framing that occur outside of the core loop of gameplay but can be extremely useful tools for providing additional narrative structure. Designers should use every moment available to them to shape the experience of a game.

One of the most common pieces of design advice is to start the game when the turns get interesting. This is similar to the narrative concept of starting a story *in medias res*—in the middle of the action. If a game should begin mechanically when things get interesting, it only follows that the theme should as well. A well-knitted theme should begin with the same intensity as the mechanics.

That doesn't mean that a game can't have any exposition, however. The introductory paragraph in the rulebook gives us a chance to tell players what they are doing and why they are doing it. In general, rulebook lore is most effective when it gives context to gameplay. The entire history of your world is not only unnecessary but can be detrimental to the goal of giving players context for their actions, because by giving them too much information, you reduce the likelihood that they will absorb the important part of the lore—which is the part that connects their avatar to the action of the game. In other words, too much lore is as bad, or worse, than no lore. However, the right amount of lore can add a lot to the play experience by setting expectations for the action and tone of the game.

There are many ways of incorporating lore in rulebooks that will enhance player experiences, but I want to focus on the introductory paragraph. Specifically, I want to look at one method for introductory paragraphs that meshes well with the game design advice of jumping straight into the action: using inciting incidents. If we want games to start with rising action, one way to jump directly into the action on turn one is to have an inciting incident described in the rulebook, specifically the introductory paragraph. Another way is to have the inciting incident occur during setup.

An inciting incident is the event at the beginning of a story that sets the main characters on the path that becomes the rest of the story. What caused the avatars to act in this way? Why are they in opposition or cooperation with the other characters? Ideally, you can also use the inciting incident to explain why the main characters want what they want.

This is an especially good way to use snippets of fiction. Instead of an unconnected short story tangentially related to gameplay, an inciting incident scene at the beginning of the rulebook can propel players into the action of the game. The main caveat here is that the inciting incident should be about the characters that are in the game, not other characters in your lore, and the incident should lead directly into the action of the game. The players won't be propelled into the action of the game if the lore does not directly apply to them and what they're doing.

Inciting incidents are not the main action of the game, merely what sparks the action. As such, you really shouldn't need more than a couple paragraphs at most to set up the action of the game. In order for players to internalize the "why" of the action, the lore needs to be brief and to the point. Much in the same way that the theme provides logic for the mechanics, the introductory lore of the game should set up the logic of the theme. In the best case scenario, the player who reads the rulebook internalizes the reason for the action of the game and the motivation of the characters and relays all of that to the other players. Lore paragraphs should be opt-in, so making them memorable and relevant will help your lore proliferate among players who tend to skip opt-in elements.

A good example is *So You've Been Eaten*, a two-player, asymmetric game in which one player is a miner and the other is a giant space worm. The title itself serves as exposition, providing the setting and tone of the game. The lore is styled as training propaganda for the employee character who mines the worms:

> So, You've Been Eaten.
>
> Don't worry, this is simply an occupational hazard. In fact, it is fairly common among Deep Space Miners (5th class), and some say that it is almost unavoidable. And, well, it is. Especially since the crystals that you seek happen to be inside giant space beasts. To mine them, you need to, well, be eaten.
>
> But, no reason to panic. We are here to help you deal with the physical and mental challenges of being eaten. This handy simulation/survival guide is standard issue for all recruits and will eventually lead to a productive, if not potentially brief, career in space mining.
>
> Should you achieve your objective and mine enough crystals to meet your quota, it is then cost-effective for the company to activate your jetpack and extricate you from the proverbial belly of the beast. While the beast's immune response was not enough to prevent its demise, its contribution to human progress and corporate profitability are most definitely appreciated.
>
> In the eventuality that the bacteria present in the beast overwhelm you and you are digested, do not worry. Your non-organic parts will ultimately provide much utility to future space miners. In fact, you may encounter some such pieces of equipment in your expedition, remains of attempts by evidently less-than-qualified recruits.
>
> Finally, it could transpire that you do not collect the necessary crystals by the time you reach the end of the beast's digestive tract. In this case, the so-called "ending #2", you will then exit the beast from the other end than the one you entered. Alive, and yet forever changed. In this case, and after a thorough decontamination and quarantine period, we will have to evaluate your performance versus that of the beast's efforts to consume you.[13]

This tells us who we are and why we are doing the actions in the game, while also establishing the tone. The main thing we don't learn is why we would have signed up for this job to begin with, but this introductory lore is already on the long side, so adding more context isn't ideal.

Setup-as-inciting-incident is trickier to pull off. It is more difficult to include important story moments while learning the rules of the game. *Vengeance* is a dice-based, action movie themed game that uses setup as a series of inciting incidents. *Vengeance* has an initial draft before play starts that functions as the inciting incident for why the avatars want revenge. Importantly, the exposition of *Vengeance* is largely "you have seen revenge action movies before; you know what to expect." To have inciting incidents in setup, a game should be strongly story driven and some element of setup should be variable. Otherwise, let the lore paragraph do the heavy lifting for you rather than drag out setup for the sake of choreographed narrative. The goal of the players will always be to get into the game quickly; don't stand in the way of that goal.

Not all story-driven moments during setup will be inciting incidents, however. In my game, *Deadly Dowagers*, players choose a husband before the game starts. Different husbands grant different temporary benefits. However, the inciting incident is not the act of getting married, but the introductory scene in the rulebook where a character discovers an older woman who sets her on the path to becoming a deadly dowager. Getting married before gameplay is exposition. It establishes the current state of the game world but does not of itself kick off the action. Similarly, choosing what character you will play or their starting gear is not an inciting incident. Inciting incidents must create motivation for characters to act out the actions of gameplay.

Inciting incidents can help us frame the narrative by showing what sparked the events of a game. By placing inciting incidents in the rulebook or setup, we free up our games to start at the point when the action really gets going. Focusing introductory rulebook lore on inciting incidents rather than exposition keeps the lore focused on the action and motivation of the avatars.

EXPOSITION AND DENOUEMENT

While there are a number of ways to introduce your game world to players, I think some methods are both more straightforward and more effective forms of storytelling. In the previous section, I discussed using the introductory lore paragraph in the rulebook as an inciting incident for the narrative of gameplay. In this section, I'll be looking at using setup as exposition and scoring as denouement.[14] Not every instance of setup and endgame scoring needs to be incorporated into the theme. As discussed in Chapter 4, it may be a better design choice to leave purely agential mechanics unthemed. However, there are times when adding a layer of thematic explanation makes for a more compelling narrative.

But first, why would we want an inciting incident before exposition? When we place the inciting incident in the lore paragraph in the rulebook, it functions similarly to a cinematic cutscene at the beginning of a video game. We get dropped into a dramatic narrative moment, then we pause to learn who we are and what we are doing. In a video game, this might happen in a tutorial level. In board games, often all we have is setup.

How can setup function as exposition? Setup is when the game world is literally built on the table. You learn who you are, what you are good at, how much you possess, etc. You learn your goals. For example, in *Sheriff of Nottingham*, players are given a hand of goods, a bag representing a cart, a few coins, and a board representing a market stall. The world is described as a line of carts waiting to get through a city gate. You have limited funds that you can use to bribe the sheriff. You have the goods you are bringing to market. The law prohibits the sale of contraband at the market, but a well-placed bribe could circumvent it. The Sheriff makes money either through bribes or penalties. All of this is learned during setup. This is the game world; the player decides how honest they will be at the city gate. The inciting incident, as described in the rulebook, is that Prince John has placed the Sheriff at the gate to inspect all incoming goods. According to the lore paragraph, the merchants are overtaxed and trying to make a living, and the Sheriff is greedy. Setup, rules, and gameplay all flow together to create a single story.

Setup tells us what we need to know about the world we will be playing in. At the end of the game, scoring is an opportunity for one last narrative flourish. Not all game structures need or can accommodate a denouement. However, games with post-game scoring can have the scoring phase integrated into the theme by treating the phase as denouement. How does being the best in a category affect a character? Why would that be important to them? This is where the theme of *Sheriff of Nottingham* breaks down. Nothing in the game world explains why it is important or desirable or profitable to be the king or queen of apples, except that you get more points. The bonus points are necessary for the mechanics to feel balanced. We can make inferences about the economy, but the extra steps needed to rationalize a game rule will make the game feel less thematic even if the theme can be justified. On the other hand, the end scoring in *Canvas* has players adding up the awards their paintings have won to determine which artist has won Best in Show. This scoring system will feel thematic to anyone who has ever attended an adjudicated art show or indeed any sort of adjudicated event. In *Canvas*, players are not left wondering at the end of the game what the scoring had to do with the theme. Rather, the final score is the point of the theme.

Scoring should tie directly to the players' main goal in the game. Where possible, scoring should make sense in the overall story. The numbers themselves and the process of tabulating them do not have to exist in the game world, but the actions and resources they represent should be tied to clear goals. We should have an idea of what happens to a character in the immediate aftermath of the game: they won or lost a contest, they amassed wealth, they lost a war, etc. Board games are stories as snapshots; we won't know much about the lives of characters after a non-narrative game is over. But we should know how their position has changed from when the game began and what that might mean to them.

A board game begins at setup and ends when a winner is declared. Designers have opportunities to make their games more thematic simply by including the whole game in the theme. Every game tells a story, and I want to see designers become better storytellers.

Exercise 5.1: Pick one of your designs or a published game. Answer all the questions in the Narrative Framing section of this chapter.

Exercise 5.2: Pick one of your designs or a published game. What is the inciting incident in the narrative of the game? If you cannot find one, what would make the most sense?

Exercise 5.3: Pick one of your designs or a published game. What does the setup and rules explanation imply about the world? Are there ways to change setup that would add exposition without adding lore text?

Exercise 5.4: Pick one of your designs or a published game. What does the end game condition imply about the world? Is there a way to adjust the game ending that feels narratively connected to the theme?

NOTES

1. Slice-of-life stories or plays typically have no discernible plot, but instead simulate a view into a moment in time of a person's life in a hyper-realistic way. This style of narrative is not very common because audiences find it boring. However, similar simulations in video games are quite popular, possibly due to the degree of control players have over the environment.

2. None of the numerous versions of *Love Letter* attempt to address my complaints, to the best of my knowledge. Some depart so far from the original mechanics that they are a full redesign of the game, rather than reframing the theme into something that makes sense with the original action of the game.
3. Setting is discussed in Chapter 8.
4. Abstraction is discussed more in Chapters 7 and 10.
5. "Simulation" or "fidelity" could also be used in place of resolution, but I feel that resolution best describes the concept I express here.
6. This is where high resolution differs from well-knitted themes. A well-knitted theme can be any complexity.
7. I would point you to Chapter 4 of *Characteristics of Games* for an introduction to game arcs (George Skaff Elias, Richard Garfield, and K. Robert Gutschera, *Characteristics of Games*. Cambridge, MA: MIT press, 2012, pp. 101–136.)
8. Tim Fowers' anticipation arc model is an in-depth take on game arcs from a player experience perspective. (Tim Fowers, "Anticipation w/ Tim Fowers," YouTube video, posted by "Tabletop Network," March 7, 2021, https://www.youtube.com/watch?v=FnmpGqOxM4Y.)
9. A good but short description of scene work can be found in Chapter 26 of *Acting One* by Robert Cohen (Robert Cohen, "Scene Structure," In *Acting One*, Boston, MA: McGraw-Hill Higher Education, 2007, p. 225.)
10. If this all sounds like I am describing mechanical game arcs and not narrative, that is because acting and game design employ such similar language.
11. Chapters 6 and 7 take two different looks at motivation and player investment.
12. The rules of narrative writing come into play when a game is text heavy. I am ignoring this wrinkle because advice on shaping traditional narrative is abundant.
13. LudiCreations, "So, You've Been Eaten," *Board Game Geek*, March 15, 2021, https://boardgamegeek.com/boardgame/284842/so-youve-been-eaten.
14. I am assuming that setup includes at minimum a brief rules overview.

REFERENCES

1. Elias, George Skaff, Richard Garfield, and K. Robert Gutschera. *Characteristics of Games*. Cambridge, MA: MIT Press, 2012.
2. Fowers, Tim. "Anticipation w/ Tim Fowers." YouTube video. Posted by "Tabletop Network," March 7, 2021. https://www.youtube.com/watch?v=FnmpGqOxM4Y.
3. Cohen, Robert. "Scene Structure," In *Acting One*, edited by Janet M. Beatty, Jennifer Mills, and Margaret Moore, 225–233. Boston, MA: McGraw-Hill Higher Education, 2007.
4. LudiCreations. "So, You've Been Eaten." *Board Game Geek*. March 15, 2021. https://boardgamegeek.com/boardgame/284842/so-youve-been-eaten.

GAMES REFERENCED

Puerto Rico
Puerto Rico 1897
Love Letter
Through the Ages: A New Story of Civilization
Antike II
Passing Through Petra
Small World
Forgotten Waters
Space Base
So You've Been Eaten
Vengeance
Deadly Dowagers
Sheriff of Nottingham
Canvas

CHAPTER 6

Building Characters

Chapter 4 introduced the idea of the avatar as the thematic representation of the player in the game. This chapter and the next explore ways to make more deeply thematic avatars.

AVATAR TEMPLATES

When developing themes alongside mechanics, an important question to ask is "Who are the players' avatars in the game?" Most, but not all, thematic games benefit from an explicit answer to that question. However, types of avatar characters require different considerations. I divide board game character archetypes or roles into six categories.

The Hero

The Hero is probably the first role most people think of. Hero characters may be solo acts (especially in competitive or solo games), team members (such as in cooperative games), or faction leaders (skirmish and civilization games). This role requires that you know specifically who you are playing and that that role is in some way unique from the other players. Characters may have different stats or powers, but different portraits can be enough of a distinction. Unique jobs can also be enough. If the job is carpenter and every player is playing the same nameless, faceless carpenter, that job will not make players feel like they are the hero of their story. However, being the only stone mason in the village is enough detail to become invested in the life of a character. And in fact, most games where players play only one character will provide some thematic detail about

DOI: 10.1201/9781003453765-8

the characters, either via text or illustration. Importantly, a character is not always a person; sometimes your character is a corporation or other entity. As long as a corporation has a unique logo and/or player power, it is still within the hero role.[1]

The Baddie

The Baddie could be a villain character or a traitor character.[2] Villains are bad from the outset, while traitor characters often switch sides at some point during the game. Villains, as a role distinct from heroes, are opposed to the majority of players, such as in one-vs-all games. To be a villain, the character must be in opposition to the other characters in a way that those characters are not in opposition to each other. A thematically villainous character could still fill the role of hero, if they are not uniquely opposed to the other characters. Additionally, baddies should, in general, be outnumbered by other characters. Even teams of heroes and baddies do not have the same oppositional experience, playing instead like any number of other faction or team-based games. Villain roles often give their players more information, or exclusive information, that is hidden from the other characters, such as in hidden movement games. Narratively, this gives the role a "plotting" feel. Villain roles may require a player to curate the experience for the other players rather than play as competitively as possible. Villains need the same level of detail that heroes do in order for players to invest in them as characters, but because they follow different rules in order to be considered in this category, the minimum required level of detail comes built into the role.

The Boss

The Boss could be a business manager, a general, or even a deity, depending on what makes sense in the fiction, but they are not generally specified characters. This role is what happens when you don't specify a hero character, but the player-controlled characters clearly don't have free will. This role is common in worker placement games and asymmetrical games. If a manager, general, or deity has a named role and card art, that technically makes them a hero (or villain) character and not a boss. The boss is a meta-explanation for why the player has total control over a number of drone-like characters. In *Agricola*, a worker placement game about family subsistence farms, the boss character is implied to be the head of the family. In city-building games like *Everdell*, players can be assumed to be mayors approving building projects or project foremen, as is the case in *The Pillars of the Earth* in which players control teams of workers but are all working on the same cathedral. Boss characters are implied when the game states that each player is or controls a group of characters. Because players make decisions from a single, somewhat omniscient perspective, a decision-making character is implied.

The Squad

The Squad could be a team, a family, or other small group. In this situation, the player is playing as multiple characters. In many games with multiple avatars per player, there is an implied boss character (a Boss) or an explicit leader (a Hero). However, in games like *Flamme Rouge* or *The Quest for El Dorado*, you can definitely make the case that while the player has god-level control and knowledge in the game, the characters in the story are presumed to have free will. This is easier to do if the characters have separate goals, abilities, or trajectories that can narratively imply independent decision-making. I would also argue that fewer characters work better when implying free will. In both of the following examples, the squads in the game consist of two characters. In *Flamme Rouge*, the avatars are differentiated by the type of cycler they are. Each player controls a pace-setting cyclist and a sprinter. The two cyclists have different decks of cards that control the speed of the cyclist. As a result, players feel as though they are controlling two genuinely different characters, who take exhaustion and burst ahead at different moments of the game. In *The Quest for El Dorado*, players control explorers racing to be the first to get to El Dorado. In the main mode of the game, players take on a hero role, but in the two-player variant, players control a squad of two explorers. Unlike *Flamme Rouge*, the explorers are controlled by a single deck of cards. However, in *El Dorado*, explorers aren't tied to a specific route and can meander across a hex map. In this case, the members of the squad feel unique because they can have different short-term goals determined by the player sending them in different directions across the map. There are also other characters represented in the cards of the game, but those cards are used as resources and thematically are not group leaders unlike the pawns on the map. Squad roles should fundamentally feel as though a player has decided to play more than one character at once, but designed in such a way that the rules of doing so do not become a burden.

Blind Forces

Blind Forces fall somewhere between the hero and the boss. Players may be told who they are, but who they are is a force of nature, a law of physics, or a philosophical idea. Players may be mechanically distinct from one another, but won't have much in the way of character background.[3] Storytelling can get tricky around blind forces, as players won't have discernible in-world motivation to defeat other players. An example is *Petrichor*, an area majority game in which players play clouds who have a preference for what kind of crops their water grows.

Unspecified Roles

Unspecified Roles are sometimes the best options. Sometimes, the implications of a role take your worldbuilding in a direction you don't want it to go. For example, if you try to figure out who your avatar is in *A Fistful of Meeples*, a mancala-style worker placement game, you may come to the conclusion that you are an Old West mobster extorting a town. In the game, players control robbers, builders, miners, and deputies. The income from the miners, deputies, and robbers flows to the players based on the actions they took on their turns. On the same turn, a player might benefit from a robbery and an arrest. Instead of trying to justify this mechanism, the game wisely doesn't try to explain why you benefit from both arrests and robberies. In other games, the most logical explanation is either boring or doesn't add much to the game. I think of these as "filing clerk" roles. An example is *Space Base*, where your role is specified in the rules fluff and never again—because you are a garage attendant for a space station. The boss role is a subtype of unspecified roles, but one that players could intuitively explain after playing your game in a way that makes thematic sense. Another subtype of unspecified roles is when players are playing agentially. Players will sometimes take on the role of "player performing a mechanical action" that is not tied into the theme. Because the action is not tied into the theme, the role is not either. This is related to the agential game state discussed in Chapter 4.

Roles are a huge aspect of worldbuilding. Mechanically, roles provide logic for player actions. Thematically, roles allow players to invest in their characters. Roles should be consistent with the logic of your worldbuilding. Often it is better to specify the roles your players will take on in your game, but you may find that this creates more narrative problems than it solves, in which case you may choose to leave the player role unspecified.

DEGREES OF MOTIVATIONAL EXCHANGE

In the book *Games: Agency as Art*, C. Thi Nguyen discusses the submersion of players into a game as the taking on of temporary agencies. He makes the claim that players take on temporary motivations or "disposable ends" when they play games which they drop when the game is over.[4] I take his line of thinking a step further by breaking down the various ways this submersion into a game is expressed in board games through different ways players interface with the theme of a game.

When you sit down to play a game, there are a number of ways you might interact with it on a thematic level. I have addressed the avatar roles common in board games in the previous section, which overlap somewhat with this topic, but avatar roles are more directly theme-focused. Players can interface with avatar roles to varying degrees of connectivity or submersion into a character. The more "in character" a player acts—via the game rules or meta-roleplaying—the more motivational exchange has occurred. Motivational exchange is simply when a player temporarily assumes the motivations of their character. The greater the degree of the exchange, the more the player will identify with the character throughout play. Degrees of motivational exchange are player-focused rather than theme-focused, which is to say that the same avatar role category could fall into multiple categories of motivational exchange depending on how it is executed within a certain game.

When playing a thematic game, players may take on the motivation to achieve not only the mechanical goals but also the game world goals. One result of taking on temporary motivations is that players may become more emotionally invested in the fate of their characters beyond just what is needed to win the game. I don't want to dwell too much on whether you, as a designer, have control over whether a player engages in roleplaying or not. Rather, I think it is useful to ask what degree of motivational exchange a game encourages in players and whether or not most players engage at that level. I identify four broad categories of motivational exchange; however, you may prefer to break the last category into two or more types when analyzing a design.

Pure Agent

In agential-only motivational exchange, players do not interface with their avatars at all motivationally. In abstract games and games with layered-on themes, players will assume the motivation of the mechanical game objectives only. Players may also assume agential-only motivation if they are highly competitive by focusing exclusively on mechanical strategies and win conditions. In thematic games, players may choose not to assume thematic motivations if they dislike the theme. Lastly, if players have played the game enough that the theme recedes into the background, they may no longer assume thematic motivations even if they did in early plays.[5] A pure agent is the floor of motivational exchange. If a player does not assume the mechanical goals of the game while playing, they arguably could be considered to have not played the game at all.

Unseen Operator

In thematic games with players controlling multiple characters—especially if the players have "unspecified" roles—the players may assume the motivations of the characters in a very surface level way. The players act as puppet masters of the characters and may sacrifice the goals of one character in order to secure the overall goal of the game. In *Village*, players control villagers going about their daily lives. However, periodically players are required to kill one of their villagers. (Thematically they die of old age.) Players have a choice of which villager dies. We can assume that thematically the villager did not choose their death, but rather that the player made the best agential choice available. The unseen operator in *Village* is at cross purposes to the individual characters. This level of exchange can also occur when a player is only controlling a single character, but that is less common (and more easily avoided if your goal is aligning player motivation with avatar motivation).

Self-Insert Character

"Self-insert" is a loaded term in the creative writing world, but in board games, it is frequently the ideal level of motivational exchange. As in the previous two categories, players still act as themselves, but they act within the thematic bounds of the game. At this level, a player becomes Player+, a motivationally enhanced version of themself. At the simplest level, players may not be fully aware of who their characters are, such as in *Sushi Go!* where players take on the role of customers in a sushi restaurant. When rulebooks say things such as "you are the customer," that is often a sign of a self-insert character, as opposed to games that provide character pawns or illustrated portraits to represent the characters. Games with self-insert characters use the player to represent the character. Some games make self-insert characters a way to deepen the simulative experience of the game by drawing the players into the game world. *Keep Talking and Nobody Explodes* is a digital-hybrid real time game in which players attempt to defuse a bomb. In *Keep Talking and Nobody Explodes*, you don't just care about winning the game. You take on the temporary motivation of defusing a bomb through a combination of simulative and literal actions. This is often the maximum level of thematic engagement that players who dislike roleplaying will tolerate in board games. Many people play board games because they don't like roleplaying, acting, or having to pretend to be someone else. You can, however, still transport them just as thoroughly into the theme with self-insert characters, depending on other player preference factors such as how expressive the game requires players to be. Self-insert characters will almost always fulfill the hero role.

Avatar Identification/Embodiment

This category may actually be two or more categories, but I'm declaring it a single spectrum of identification that is distinct from the other categories. When a player identifies with a character, they may begin to make game decisions that are not conducive to winning the game. Instead, they may choose to take narratively satisfying actions. Or if the character goals closely align with the player goals, they may gradually "become" the character, increasingly engaging in roleplaying over the course of the game. The deepest level of motivational exchange is adopting a temporary personality that aligns with the temporary goals of the avatar. This can be expressed through roleplaying, but often roleplaying is a conscious choice. Avatar identification may not always be a conscious choice, but rather the emotional by-product of a well-designed thematic experience. However, this does require a level of openness to the possibility of deep motivational exchange on the part of the player. I believe that this level of exchange is best handled by giving players hints at characters' personalities through mechanisms and art (along with tightly knit game goals), then letting the players assume the level of motivational exchange that they are comfortable with. In order to achieve avatar identification, players must be clear on what character they are, what that character wants, and what it might mean to them to achieve their goals.

How is motivational exchange relevant to designers? If you want your players to have a certain experience, for example thematic "immersion," one element to look at is how players interface with their avatars.

Controlling multiple units as a player may hinder thematic transportation unless players also have a single leader character with comprehensible goals and desires. Self-insert characters have thematic limits that an avatar character does not: the limits of what we can imagine ourselves doing as opposed to the actions of a fictional character. There is also the possibility of moving between categories of motivational exchange as players learn more about who they are playing as, although that is more challenging to achieve in a board game compared to TTRPGs and video games.[6] Certainly, agential motivation is still present when the game world pauses for moments of game state upkeep.

Hopefully, the next time a playtester asks you, "Who are we in this game?" you will have a better understanding of the answer (although you should give your playtesters a more straightforward response).

THEMATIC PLAYER STRATEGIES

Chapter 4 discusses how designers can connect thematic goals and mechanical actions by grouping actions into goal-related categories. Thematic goals are only the first step to a well-knitted theme and interesting game narrative. This section looks at how the types of actions the players take can influence the types of characters and stories present in a game.

Player strategies are emergent styles of gameplay that ideally lead to winning the game. Games consist of goals and obstacles, and strategies are how players attempt to overcome obstacles to reach a goal. Stories are also made up of goals, obstacles, and characters who strive with them.[7] So it makes sense when designing a thematic game to consider mechanical strategies as thematic opportunities. Probably, the easiest way to handle theming strategies is to design player powers that lean into specific strategies and assign each power a character who has a motivation for pursuing that strategy. Another way would be to have thematic endgame achievements for employing particular strategies which any character could pursue. When playtesting, observe the types of strategies used by players and see if you can develop in-world reasons for why the characters behave that way.

I have compiled a list of player strategies (and a few tactics) that you might encounter or purposely design into your game.[8] The strategies are grouped into optimization, misdirection, defense, and timing categories. I've listed thematic considerations in the descriptions of the strategies, but

I leave you to figure out how they could work narratively in your game world.

Optimization Strategies

Optimization strategies can be divided into two overall types: positive optimization and negative optimization. Most games have at least one type of optimization strategy.

Positive Optimization is the strategy of getting the highest possible value from each of your turns. Often games that encourage positive optimization will not contain other viable strategies. When there are other strategies, they can feel out of place, like "take that"—the term used to describe attacking an opponent in a non-combat game—in a resource management game. Examples of positive optimization include drawing extra cards on a turn, maximizing resource production, selling high, and timing payouts to buy low. Positive optimization is usually found in efficiency puzzles or cyclical structures. Themes that blend well with positive optimization include almost any type of technology or production, including farming.

Negative Optimization is the strategy of reducing the scope of your opponent's options for their turn. Both positive and negative optimization are a form of action economy, a term I learned from Matthew Colville's YouTube channel.[9] Colville uses action economy to describe combat balance in *Dungeons and Dragons*, which dovetails nicely with negative optimization. This isn't merely a "take that" strategy. Rather this strategy is mostly found in combat games or survival games, where you can kill/damage/capture resources or characters that your opponent uses to generate actions. The simplest example is a squad-based skirmish game, where if you kill off some of the opposing force, their options become more limited on their turn. However, casting a slow spell or imposing some other negative condition could have a similar effect of worsening the action economy of your opponent. A scorched earth strategy would be an extreme form of negative optimization. Negative optimization is always found in open conflict games and any game that involves blocking action spaces. *Citadels* is a covert conflict game that has two roles that negatively impact other players' action economies. One of the roles makes another character lose a turn and the other steals another character's gold. Themes that include negative optimization should be amenable to avatar conflict; in the case of

Citadels, the negative optimization roles are assassin and thief, which are thematically appropriate.

The following strategies are subtypes of positive and/or negative optimization strategies[10]:

- Raising the Floor is a type of positive optimization that involves improving your base economy or statistics. This strategy focuses on long-term goals over short-term gains. An example is moving up the income track in *Space Base*. When you spend currency in *Space Base*, you can only spend money up to the amount of your currency track, but then your currency marker drops to the level of your income marker, even if that means you didn't actually "spend" any money to buy a card. Raising your income ensures you always have some money regardless of the occasional bad turn. Themes for raising the floor could be economic in nature or emphasize mechanical or physical improvements—such as going to the gym to raise your strength score.
- Specialization is the focus on a single path within a game. It is often a style of positive optimization, but sometimes players may want to specialize for reasons other than optimization, especially in games where specialization isn't the best path to victory. This strategy could also be negative optimization if used to cut other players off from a type of resource. Specialization allows players to identify with their character's career, such as "pig farmer" or "cloth merchant." Roles, objectives, or achievements can further allow players to invest in their character's business successes or failures. Rewarding specialization strategies can help characters feel different from each other.
- "A Boat in Every Port" is an optimization strategy through the spreading out of your forces. This is the opposite of specialization. While most likely positive optimization, it could be a negative optimization strategy to claim resources or opportunities before your opponents can. Rarely will spreading out result in total dominance, rather this approach often gets rewarded when coming in second place enough times allows for a cumulative first place finish, for example in *Pandemic: Contagion*, a game where players earn points by having the most, second most, or third most cubes on cards. Focusing too much on having the most cubes on a card earns fewer

points than having the second most on several cards. This strategy may also put pressure on other players to go after opportunities before they planned, which could put them off balance. Business-related themes—like market penetration—work well here, as do more abstract concepts like viral spread (of either kind of virus).

- Denial is a form of negative optimization built around neutralizing your opponent's powers.[11] "Counterspells," "take that" mechanics, and blocking are all forms of denial. Themes can emphasize defensiveness or battlefield control powers for characters that make use of denial strategies.
- Gang Up On the Leader is a negative optimization strategy that is employed by players to prevent the player in the lead from winning. This is a more extreme form of denial that usually involves multiple players cooperating. Often this strategy results in a lengthened gameplay time beyond what is optimal to the experience. *King of Tokyo* is a game where the central mechanism is "king of the hill" which forces all players to adopt some form of the strategy of "gang up on the leader." Interestingly, not only does the game feature a rotating one vs. all mechanism, but it also allows players to force a player that is in the lead onto the "hill" in order to attempt to eliminate them. This strategy works well with highly combative themes.

Misdirection Strategies

Misdirection strategies seek to signal to your opponent that you aren't a threat and can be safely ignored. Games with covert conflict, particularly social deduction games, benefit from misdirection strategies. While not an example of a strategy listed below, in *Bang*! a deputy could attack the sheriff in an attempt to convince the other players that the deputy is on the same team as the outlaws.

- "Keep Your Head Down" is a strategy of quietly earning points or completing objectives in such a way that no one notices when you take the lead. While this can manifest as players being physically quiet, mechanically it can look like unflashy play styles and gradual progress. This strategy is often seen in games with open conflict but alternate win conditions. In *King of Tokyo*, the player who goes after victory points rather than damage can sometimes eke out a surprise victory if other players are not paying attention. However, like in *King of Tokyo*, going for gradual points will often be the least thematic part of a design. While it would make the tone of the game darker, the "rolling for victory points" strategy in *King of Tokyo* could have been themed around eating bystanders: the more you eat, the more points you get. While a "keep your head down" strategy crops up in other styles and structures of games, it is commonly an "above the table" strategy of keeping quiet, particularly when there isn't an alternate win condition involved. "Keep your head down" blends well with diplomatic or pacifist themes when paired with conflict in games.

- Intentional Underdog is a strategy of hanging back behind the leader. This could be to take advantage of catch-up mechanics in order to sling shot ahead or to avoid being targeted by other players. Intentional underdog is distinct from "keep your head down," because "keep your head down" is about getting ahead while no one notices, but intentional underdog is about artificially putting on the brakes to stay out of the lead. Theming your catch-up mechanics and placement bonuses and penalties could give players in-character reasons for employing this strategy.

- Sandbagging is when a player hoards resources only to convert them into points at the last possible moment. When a player sandbags, their true standing is obscured for most of the game. In this strategy, the player is never truly behind but only appears to be. Sandbagging is more common in resource management games while intentional underdog is more common in conflict games, but there is a certain amount of overlap. Sandbagging may be undesirable in a game in which case limits can be placed on the amount of resources that can be hoarded. But if the strategy is desirable, themes involving stockpiling, hoarding, or greed would be appropriate.

- Social Leveraging is a meta-strategy of convincing your opponents that you aren't a threat through persuasion, cajoling, pleading, etc. The meta-strategy aspect of not drawing attention to yourself in "keep your head down" falls into the category of social leveraging. Mechanics such as bluffing, negotiation, and trading require players to employ a certain amount of social leveraging. Social leveraging benefits from themes where characters have in-world reasons to talk to one another.

Defense Strategies

Defense strategies are about protecting yourself and your possessions. While negative optimization focuses on slowing your opponent, defensive strategies focus on dealing with hindrances and penalties that come your way.

- Turtling focuses on defensive measures at the expense of everything else. This can end up looking very similar to sandbagging, except that turtling is fairly exclusive to open conflict games. You may be familiar with this strategy if you have played *Risk* with someone who spent most of the game bunkered down in Australia building up their forces. If this strategy is desirable, you could theme a faction around paranoid isolation or a history of getting invaded.
- Weatherproofing is the strategy of always having enough resources to cover possible penalties on top of what you need to make progress in the game. This strategy could also be called "feeding your family" after the mechanism in *Agricola*, a worker placement game that requires players to feed their workers. Weatherproofing is typically a less extreme form of resource hoarding than sandbagging and has a different motivation. Themes could emphasize a character's foresight, prudence, wisdom, or even community support.
- Taking the Hit is the opposite of weatherproofing. (You could think of it as "starving your family.") This strategy can be employed in resource games with penalties or in open conflict games. In covert conflict games, you could "take one for the team" by getting eliminated to draw suspicion off of another team member. Themes could emphasize a character's willingness to sacrifice, toughness, or fearlessness.
- Cutting Your Losses focuses on retreating from a battle so as not to lose the war. *Air, Land, & Sea* is a card game that focuses on strategically withdrawing from a battle in order to win future battles. Players are attempting to control two out of three theaters of war, but can withdraw if they know they will lose a battle. Most games that

have this as a central mechanism are war-themed or structured as a "battle line" game. This strategy is mostly found in open conflict games, but also in games with betting, push your luck, or market investments. Themes could emphasize a character's business savvy, strategic brilliance, or inability to stay the course.

Timing Strategies (and Tactics)

Timing strategies and tactics are about choosing your moment or window in order to succeed. Timing strategies are so in-the-moment and often brief that you could also consider them tactics.

- Rushing the Objective focuses on achieving a goal before your opponents have time to fully power up. It is the opposite of sand-bagging. This strategy undercuts attempts at optimization, but is risky because there is usually a narrow window before a game ramps up. This strategy can be deployed in any sort of point scoring game where players control when the game ends. It can also be found in open conflict games where a player may attempt to wipe out all other players before more advanced units can be unlocked. Rushing could lead to specialization where a player has a monopoly on a resource. Themes could emphasize hastiness or greed.
- "No, After You" is a delaying tactic that attempts to force one of your opponents to make the undesirable choice. This is the strategy that occurs near the end of every round of *Azul* as players attempt to avoid taking tiles they do not have room for on their boards. This strategy also occurs in competitive games with global threats where all players could lose, but players don't want to sacrifice their turns to be the one that resolves the threat. Themes could emphasize cooperation vs. selfishness, market forces, or the downsides of innovation.
- Hail Mary is a tactic of attempting to pull a victory from the jaws of defeat. This tactic can help players feel like they still have a chance at winning, but if it succeeds too often games will feel overly random. The "You Win" card in *Space Base* can function this way. If a player was far behind on victory points, they could purchase that card as a Hail Mary. However, that card is notoriously difficult to complete before the end of the game. If you have a deus ex machina card in your game, try to tie it into your theme. Themes could emphasize rebellion, desperation, or heroism.

If the actions of a game constitute the plot elements, then player strategies are how the story gets told. A fully integrated theme will take into account how the game is played and not just what comes in the box. So much of the experience of playing a game comes from deploying different strategies. When well themed, those strategies in turn provide insight into the types of characters that inhabit the game world and the lengths they will go to get what they want.

Exercise 6.1: Make a list of your designs that made it to the playtesting stage. What roles do the players take on in the games? Would changing the types of roles help players feel more invested in the game worlds?

Exercise 6.2: List one published game for each motivational exchange type. Don't use the examples provided in the section. (If this exercise is difficult for you, pick three games and determine what type of motivational exchange is found in each.)

Exercise 6.3: Pick one of your designs or a published game that you have played. List some of the strategies in the game. Do the types of strategies in the gameplay fit with the types of characters and goals found in the theme?

Exercise 6.4: Go through the list of player strategies and list a character trait for each strategy (try not to use adjectives found in the description). For example, "prudent" for Weatherproofing.

NOTES

1. Although you should design with the implications in mind of making a corporation the hero.
2. Baddie is the gender neutral term for bad guy. A villain is bad from the outset; a traitor turns bad. Both are baddies.
3. Personified forces with character portraits would be heroes.
4. C. Thi Nguyen. *Games: Agency as Art.* Oxford: Oxford University Press, 2020.
5. This phenomenon is discussed more in Chapter 11.
6. Indeed, many video games play with the concept of player identity, such as *Portal.* In the game, players can only see themselves obliquely. The avatar in the game is never quite self-insert but also severely limits the level of avatar identification by not letting players view their character directly.
7. In the field of acting, the term "tactics" is used to describe the ways an actor relates to goals and obstacles within a scene (Robert Cohen. *Acting One.* Boston, MA: McGraw-Hill Higher Education, 2007: 34.)
8. I've focused on non-degenerate strategies, although some of these are borderline depending on how they interact with your specific design.
9. Matthew Colville, "Using 4E to Make 5E Combat More Fun: Running the Game," YouTube video, 06:20, posted by "@mcolville," December 29, 2016, https://www.youtube.com/watch?v=QoELQ7px9ws&list=PLlUk42GiU2guNzWBzxn7hs8MaV7ELLCP_&index=29.

10. In some games, increasing your available actions will decrease other players' available actions, such as in the "a boat in every port" strategy.
11. This strategy takes its name from *Magic: The Gathering*, where the term is used to refer to actions that counter an opponent's actions.

REFERENCES

1. Nguyen, C. Thi. *Games: Agency as Art.* Oxford: Oxford University Press, 2020.
2. Cohen, Robert. Acting One. Boston, MA: McGraw-Hill Higher Education, 2007.
3. Colville, Matthew. "Using 4E to Make 5E Combat More Fun: Running the Game." YouTube video, 06:20. Posted by "@mcolville." December 29, 2016. https://www.youtube.com/watch?v=QoELQ7px9ws&list=PLlUk42GiU2guNzWBzxn7hs8MaV7ELLCP_&index=29.

GAMES REFERENCED

Agricola
Everdell
The Pillars of the Earth
Flamme Rouge
The Quest for El Dorado
Petrichor
A Fistful of Meeples
Space Base
Village
Sushi Go!
Keep Talking and Nobody Explodes
Dungeons and Dragons
Citadels
Pandemic: Contagion
King of Tokyo
Air, Land, and Sea
Azul
Magic: The Gathering
Portal

CHAPTER 7

Fleshing Out Characters

NON-NARRATIVE CHARACTERS

This chapter focuses on characters and how they can shape the narrative of a game. As a reminder, while all avatars may be considered characters, not all characters are avatars. I primarily use the term characters in this chapter to refer to all types of characters in games, not just player characters.

Creating thematically rich characters in board games will never look the same as it does in novels or movies. Much like story structure, characterization in games works differently than it does in linear entertainment. However, we can still create compelling characters in our games. The primary way we do this as designers is by expressing characterization through our mechanics, not through lore. The game is the world. The actions are how the characters meaningfully interact with the world. In order for players to invest in their avatars, the character actions must make logical sense within the narrative. As you build out your theme and characters, keep in mind that your mechanics will impact the believability of your characters and thus investment in your narrative.

You will recognize some of these principles from Chapter 5 in the section on narrative framing. This section goes into greater depth on the ways rules and mechanics can shape your characters and the game world that they inhabit. Below are a number of general principles regarding the design of characters in a game world:

DOI: 10.1201/9781003453765-9

- *A character's goal (i.e. what a character desires most) should align with their mechanical win condition.* A character may have secondary goals, values, or desires, but a character's actions must be driven by their win condition(s) to be believable. They should have a purpose in life that closely ties to the "why" of gameplay. In other words, both the player and the character should be invested in the outcome of the events of the game.
- *A character's powers/unique mechanics denote their unique values.* A person can only get better at building by spending a lot of time building things, therefore a character who is better than average at building likely values their role in society as a builder. Unless you indicate otherwise, your audience will generally assume that a character performs an action because they *choose* to.[1] Since all we know about a character is what they do in a game, we assume what they do must be important to them or to the society they live in. If a character's actions are important to them, that indicates their values, at least in part. Some characters may have actions that focus on efficiency, while others focus on brute force. How someone solves a problem says a lot about their worldview, which is why character mechanics are so foundational to a character's values.
- *Rules systems outside of individual powers indicate cultural norms.* If a thematic rule is not rationalized by physics (for example, gravity), we can assume the rule exists because of the culture within the game world. One often overlooked area where this is especially true is scoring. Scoring that does not allow a player to win by more than two points might indicate a culture steeped in notions of honor and fair play. A scoring system that only allows a player to win if they are ahead by more than two points might indicate a culture that places emphasis on merit and achievement. A theme will always feel somewhat disconnected from gameplay if the core system does not largely resemble the world it represents. My game, *Deadly Dowagers*, uses rules restrictions around income to represent the restrictive nature of Victorian society for women. Whereas many games have an income phase every round, *Deadly Dowagers* only allows players to collect on their investments during an inheritance phase.

- *Characters exist within the cultural norms of the rules and respond to them.* Characters might strive to be the best within their cultural system, or they might fight against it. Factions are the result of conflicting cultural norms between two or more groups. Factions are more believable if the values and beliefs of a faction are in direct conflict with another faction. Values and beliefs, of course, are expressed by the unique mechanics of a faction. *Root* displays this concept beautifully. In *Root*, players control asymmetric factions striving for dominance in an anthropomorphic woodland setting. You don't need to read the lore for *Root* to understand the values and friction of the factions; all of that is present in the mechanics. The Eyrie Dynasties place value on tradition, which is expressed through a programming mechanic. Programming, like tradition, is slow to change in the face of new information. Their isolation to one spot on the board shows how their previous power has waned and contracted. Their history and values shine through during setup and rules explanation, only to be reinforced by gameplay. *Root* also displays a shining example of faction friction with the Marquise de Cat and the Woodland Alliance. You only need to glance from the sawmills to the faction named the "Woodland" Alliance to see the conflict brewing. The fact that the sawmills are being built by cats and that the Alliance are small prey creatures only underscores the conflict. So we end up with a faction that prizes industry above the homes and lives of others, a faction bound by tradition, and a faction inherently weaker that must rely on coalition building. The final faction in the base game is the Vagabond, a character who works outside of the rule of law, much the same way he operates outside of the lines on the map. The written lore merely exists to explicitly state and underscore what is shown in gameplay.[2] Irrelevant surface details are fine to include in written lore, but those should be sparing and as much as possible should be used to add texture to your game world by being congruous with the setting.

Agendas

How do we make a character's goals mechanics-oriented as well as thematic? I like to think of it as giving my characters agendas. For character design purposes, I define an agenda as an alignment of desires with goals, which drives a character to take action. A character doesn't just need goals or desires; they need an agenda. An agenda will compel them to take actions to achieve their goals. Those actions make up the game.

Agendas imply desires, goals, and personality traits. A list of personality traits does not make a character. Give a character an agenda and the player will be able to imagine the personality of the character on their own. Agendas don't have to be rational to the players as long as they make sense within the game mechanics. However, certain agendas will resonate more strongly with some players than others.[3]

Agendas aren't just what a character wants but why they want it. The agenda in *Agricola* is both to be prosperous and to keep your family from starving. The characters don't have much in the way of personality, but the real need to eat makes those workers feel more like characters than many other farming-themed games. In this example, the agenda gives the characters a driving purpose for their actions. "Survive" and "acquire resources'" are two of the most common agendas in games. Competing agendas can create conflict between characters, especially if the agendas are mutually exclusive. Mostly, agendas will be tied to win conditions, but as we see with the starvation mechanism *Agricola*, agendas may be tied to shorter term goals.

Giving your characters agendas is the bare minimum, however. The goal should be to give them interesting agendas. I am a fan of what I call "thinking sideways." To explain this method, I first have to explain how I build characters in *Dungeons and Dragons 5e*. If you play D&D long enough, you will eventually have to make a character solely to fill a gap in your party's composition. You will build a character that works mechanically and fits in the world, but has no personality. Fortunately, the *Player's Handbook* has personality trait tables that you can roll on to give you direction for roleplaying your character. The chapter on backgrounds provides lists of traits, bonds, ideals, and flaws that are associated with a number on a die.[4] By rolling a die on each table, you will generate a combination of personality traits for your character. Each type of background has its own tables with suggestions unique to that background. Unfortunately, the tables are filled with overdone tropes that don't really help make a character with the nuance I'm looking for. This is where thinking sideways comes into play. I usually choose a background for my character based on what abilities it grants me rather than as backstory fodder. However, early in my roleplaying career, I was rolling for traits, ideals, and bonds and noticed how unexpectedly interesting my results were. I then realized that I was looking at the wrong tables for my chosen background and was instead rolling on the tables of the previous background that were on the facing page. The results were interesting because they were no longer generic fantasy tropes when coupled with the "wrong" background. The traits now suggested a unique and interesting character.[5]

By looking sideways to adjacent character tropes and using them outside of their expected context, I can create better characters. Sometimes that means changing the agenda and sometimes that means changing the character. For example, I can take a stock supervillain and give them a family they need to protect. Magneto is interesting not because he is evil, but because he has an agenda that's tied to emotions that are comprehensible to viewers.

On the other hand, I can recast a character to better fit an agenda I want in my game. I recast my game about inheriting estates that featured multiple generations of aristocratic men and replaced them with murderous women who marry for wealth. *Deadly Dowagers* is still about accruing wealth and moving up the nobility ladder. The core mechanics didn't change very much when the change was made, but over time, the new agenda shaped the development of the game. The immediate change was that the game became more interesting because the cast was more interesting. Not simply because the characters are now women instead of men; that would be an art choice by itself. No, it is because the characters have a more interesting agenda. "Become rich and powerful over the course of generations" is an agenda that has been used in many games before. "Take matters into your own hands in spite of societal and moral objections" is a much more interesting agenda.

If you are designing a fantasy-themed game, write out a breakdown of a typical "fantasy adventuring party." Then shuffle the traits around. Now, you won't be able to call someone an archer if they don't use a bow. But maybe dwarves with longbows and elves with axes can spark ideas for ways to develop your world in a unique direction. This same process can work in a lot of genres of games and is especially good for art direction. But don't discount the thematic and mechanical interplay of giving characters agendas and personalities by relying solely on art.

A note on character personalities: I describe the characters in *Deadly Dowagers* as murderous because that adjective describes their actions during gameplay. A character who regularly donates to religious charities could be described as charitable or pious. I would avoid most personality descriptors that relate to mood—cranky, bubbly, gloomy, sunny—or those that relate to appearance. Show; don't tell. Your character's appearance belongs in their illustration. Your character's mood might appear in dialogue, if there is any. If there isn't any dialogue, I would suggest showing mood through the art as well.

Why do your characters want to win? What is at stake for them? What are they willing to give up to succeed? How do their agendas conflict with other characters and with the world around them? At the very least, this method should make your characters more memorable, which hopefully transfers to a more memorable game.

CREATING PLAYER INVESTMENT THROUGH CHARACTER MOTIVATION

The previous section discusses the concept of agendas and how a character's desires need to align with their goals and actions. This section dives into how a character's desires can function as the connecting point between an avatar and a player by providing agendas that are motivating to players.

Often, when we talk about designing for player experience, we focus on how we want the players to feel. However, emotional responses are the end result of our design choices, not a starting point. There are many different ways of crafting experience depending on what type of game you are designing. It is possible to guess the emotional experiences your players will have based on how your game is structured.[6] Starting with how we want players to react to our designs is difficult when we are still in the idea generation phase; we can instead start from a more concrete place. In this section, I'm going to look at one approach to crafting experiences for thematic games: character motivation.

When attempting to create emotional resonance within a theme, my design goal is to create investment in players' in-game actions.[7] Player investment gives me wiggle room with regard to particular emotions rather than attempting to design for a specific set of emotions. If players are invested, the game actions will take on an importance beyond what is needed to win the game. In other words, they will be motivated by their investment to play in the game world. All I need to do is supply the motivation.

On the surface, motivation is as sticky a topic as emotion, but I think it is more actionable. Emotion is the end result of an action; it is responsive. Motivation is the trigger to take an action. I can playtest my way to desired emotions in a design, but that doesn't help guide my initial game idea toward an emotionally resonant theme. Different people will react to stimuli in different ways, and not everyone finds the same emotional experiences enjoyable. However, there is some evidence that we all operate with similar motivations.

Steven Reiss, an American psychologist, developed a list of 16 basic human desires that make up human motivation. Those motivations are romance, curiosity, honor, acceptance, order, family, independence, power, social contact, physical activity, status, saving (desire to collect), eating, vengeance, tranquility, and idealism.[8] This is a robust list, but it does leave off some of the basic bodily functions that we are also motivated by. We can add some of Maslow's needs to round out this list for our purposes: physiological needs (such as breathing and sleep) and safety (protection from elements or injury).[9] How does this list help with theme crafting?

We all experience similar drives. Whether the list in the previous paragraph is infallible on a scientific level does not matter because in general we recognize that actions can be motivated by the desires on the list. If the characters we play also exhibit those drives, we will become invested in the action. We become invested because the action is comprehensible to us; we know why someone would want to act and what drives them to action. This is true even if we don't agree ethically or strategically with the actions taken by the characters. To be believable, it is enough that we understand the motivation. We would not declare war on our neighbor, but the desire for more power is comprehensible to us and allows us to become invested in a combat game.

In order to be effective, motivation must spring from the game mechanisms. We cannot simply tell players their motivation and assume that will be enough. But how do we show motivation through mechanisms? Motivation is expressed via mechanical goals or rules restrictions. As a type of goal, motivation should be paired with an obstacle that directly threatens the goal. The desire for independence springs from my autonomy being threatened. The desire for order becomes stronger when there are limits on how I can create order. Ideally, motivational goals and obstacles should be reinforced by thematic labeling of the characters. The actions a motivated character takes in a game are the results of their desires, and the combination of actions and desires indicates their identity within the world. As designers, we can indicate identity to players by giving characters job titles that match their motivation. *Ex Libris*, a worker placement tableau-building game, presents the desire for order to great effect by putting restrictions on how you can order cards and then making the characters librarians. Many games have tableau building with restrictions on where you can place cards; this is not innovative. *Ex Libris* makes its tableau building both comprehensible and emotionally resonant by providing avatars whose job is keeping books in order. Players can get upset when a card they need to fill out a shelf is taken by another player, even if the points that card would confer wouldn't help the player that much. This is because players become invested in the alphabetizing aspect of the theme as it is thematically accessible to players who have been in libraries but are not librarians, but also because filling in a row fulfills our innate desire for order. I imagine that professional librarians would find the curation of types of books to be equally thematic, but this mechanism puts less pressure on our intrinsic motivation. It is the combination of motivation based on the universal human desire for order and a rationale for that motivation (you are a librarian) that produces the investment in the theme.

Rules restrictions can create additional goals for players by threatening consequences if they don't meet the restrictions. A builder might need to eat every round or become weaker. A soldier might need to acquire armor or risk injury. Rules restrictions create secondary goals and obstacles in addition to the win condition, which can provide motivations that are in tension with the primary motivation. In *Deep Sea Adventure*, a "push your luck" game, players are treasure-hunting divers who must return to the submarine before they run out of air. Players are collecting treasure but are limited in how far they can travel forward by how much they are already carrying. The basic motivation is saving (or collecting). The air mechanism adds the physiological need to breathe as a motivation-and-goal with the obstacle being the finite amount of air available to the divers. Finally, the competitive nature of the game adds the motivation of status—players want to win by collecting the most treasure, therefore the avatars must desire that as well.

How do we build motivation into our characters? First, we must ask what types of actions and goals are present in a game. Then, we have to identify what drives a character to seek those goals and take those actions.

We must apply obstacles to the goals which will reinforce the motivation. (Conversely, we could select a motivation that is reinforced by the obstacles already in our design and build out the theme from there.) Finally, we can signify our characters' motivations by labeling the actions, goals, obstacles, and characters in a way that further reinforces the theme established by the design itself. *Ex Libris* would have a less accessible theme if the characters were *not* librarians.

When I play or design a thematic game, I am quick to ask, "Why should I care?" What is appealing about the action of the characters? Would I find that action satisfying in play? Does that action make sense in the world of the theme? You don't need to do a lot of world building to create player investment in theme. You just need to align character motivation with action in a way that resonates with players.

A PRACTICAL LOOK AT EVIL CHARACTERS

This section is included here because it is a specific look at a particular issue but also outlines an important step in the theme-building process, that of considering the message implied by the theme.

I'm concluding this discussion of characters with the thorny problem of evil avatars in non-narrative games. What qualifies as evil, especially in a non-narrative game? The problem with discussing villains is that the discussion can swing wildly from creative writing techniques to real-world ethics—whether or not the person speaking is qualified to speak about ethics. So, let's set a simple definition for the sake of this discussion and try not to wade too deep into topics I'm not qualified to talk about. Let's define fictional evil as intentional harm to others for selfish or other immoral reasons.

What type of evil avatars (or non-player characters) already exist in board games? There is a whole spectrum, but most people tend to think about the supervillains and forget the others. Disney and comic book villains are at the less evil end of the spectrum.[10] We don't see much of their motivation in gameplay and these games are typically family friendly. As a result, the actions of the heroes and villains do not feel very different from one another, morally. Similarly, there are faction-based games that have clear good and bad sides, but that lore knowledge comes from an outside source (e.g. any *Lord of the Rings* game where you can play as orcs). Anti-hero avatars, such as in any heist game, tend to have a clearly selfish motivation, but the harm they do is typically either non-violent or violent against someone who is portrayed as more evil than the avatar. Sometimes, the baddies aren't more evil than the good characters, but instead are secretly part of a faction with a hidden, ulterior motivation. These games may end in a betrayal, but if the betrayal is not for immoral or selfish reasons, then the character is not evil by our definition.[11] Finally, we have characters that are clearly evil based on their actions within the game. These characters are the trickiest to design well and thus are the characters I will focus my attention on.

A believably evil character has goals and few moral compunctions about how they reach those goals. Not every game has the ability to showcase a character's values and motivation during gameplay.[12] As mentioned above, recognizable characters are able to lean on outside sources to establish why the baddies are bad. However, this means that your game must make sense within that larger context. If the Sauron in your game is trying to amass gold and dominate trade routes, any preexisting knowledge players have of *The Lord of the Rings* will only cause dissonance.

Characters that are believably evil are a tricky proposition in part because of how character is expressed in board games. Avatars perform evil acts via the actions of the players. Vile acts carry a strong emotional component for audiences. Performing these acts, even metaphorically, internalizes the moral taboo within the player. This can create situations in games that are known within the industry as "not fun." The solution is usually to rely on either abstraction or absurdity within your design, even when the theme has external sources. Abstraction and/or absurdity helps relieve that emotional stress. Think about the abstracted murders of the many Jack the Ripper themed games. An excellent example of both abstraction and absurdity is *The Bloody Inn*.[13] *The Bloody Inn* is a card game in which players are innkeepers who rob and murder their guests. In the game, murder is simply represented by moving a card to your player area. The absurdity of *The Bloody Inn* comes from the sheer number of crimes you'll be committing all while also attempting to run a profitable business. *The Bloody Inn* also uses cartoonishly macabre art to set the absurd tone of the game.

A quick note about abstraction: all board games abstract theme to a certain extent.[14] However, the type of thematic abstraction we see in *The Bloody Inn* carries weight. Instead of focusing on graphic realism, this sort of abstraction allows designers to shift the players' focus to the decisions involved in evil acts. I'm not sure whether there is much value in grossing out players or making them violate taboos, but exploring the decisions that can lead to devaluing human life, especially at an abstracted remove, is very interesting to me. Consider the difference between stage plays and movies. Plays often eschew the special effects used by movies in favor of exploring the psychology behind actions. In board games, players get to experience the pressures and choices that lead to evil acts. I think that's a great reason to make a game with evil avatars and an even greater reason to include a certain amount of abstraction of the evil acts themselves.

A game that I feel is too specific and earnest in its dark setting is *Abomination: Heir of Frankenstein*, a worker placement game in which players are mad scientists racing to be the first to successfully create a companion for Frankenstein's monster. Right off the bat, this game is much less abstracted, both in player actions and art assets. Players are committing murder and collecting body parts throughout the game. Remember, abstraction provides a mental buffer for players to not get too emotionally affected by the actions they are taking. Further, while the number and severity of crimes in *Abomination* does trend to the absurd, the game plays it straight and not for laughs. Laughter is a useful mental buffer when playing games with murder. The art style is macabre in a more serious tone, like what you would see in a grim dark RPG. Still, I think that where the game really falls down is in fumbling its source material. The serious tone and graphic nature of the game could have been forgiven if the critical theme of the external source it relied upon lined up with the action found in the game. Mary Shelley's *Frankenstein* uses the horrific setting of the book to make a point about the monstrous nature of society. In *Abomination*, you (a mad scientist) are the monstrous one, not society. The tonal mismatch means that while the external source helps you understand the context of what you are doing, it does little to address why. As a result, this game cannot rely on the source material to justify your actions.[15]

Some stories are better suited to certain forms of entertainment over others. The Sondheim musical *Assassins* is a serious exploration of evil wrapped in catchy music. The music broadens the appeal of the show, but also makes the topic feel less serious than it is. Board games, with their art and abstraction, can do the same thing but not necessarily with the same subjects. Because the main event in *Assassins* is an act of terroristic violence that takes place in living memory, it would be a terrible board game. Tabletop games are about player interactivity. When considering evil characters of history performing evil actions in a game, a certain amount of historical distance is necessary for players. *Deadly Dowagers* goes a step further by not having historical figures/real people depicted at all, while still using historical distance. Asking players to perform evil acts is one thing when those acts are fictional and absurd. Asking players to decide to commit terrorism in a game moves that game into the "serious games" genre if done extremely well, but is more likely to come across as extremely poor taste.

The act of play is not truly separate from the real world. We bring our morals and ethics and histories with us into play. When a game offers a moral choice, our first instinct is to act according to our own morals. This can be overridden if we go into the game with a clear plan to act other than how we normally would. How the particular game is pitched or framed will also have an affect on our actions. Even if expectations are set, there are certain issues to take into account. There are levels to how bad an evil action will feel depending on a number of variables, such as the level of abstraction, the art, and nature of the action. Asking a player to literally lie to another player (such as in *Sheriff of Nottingham*) is a hard "no" for some of my friends. Asking characters to make evil decisions has a broader appeal and fewer pitfalls than asking them to perform evil actions.

Evil characters must have comprehensible agendas. If you are going to design a game with evil avatars, you really need to have either internal or external sources for motivation that are clear and congruous with the experience of gameplay. *The Bloody Inn* succeeds because we believe that the characters are greedy and that their greed drives them to commit horrific crimes. Even with external sources, *Abomination* fails at character motivation. "Because you want to be like Dr. Frankenstein" is a poor motivation based on the source material (spoiler alert: he dies) and the motivation used in the game, "because the monster is forcing me to do it," is even worse as it is not a motivation at all.[16] Better motivators for evil acts would be single word traits, such as pride, ambition, greed, or revenge. These traits can be made explicit through a character's actions throughout the game. One of the actions in *The Bloody Inn* is money laundering, which seems mostly to exist to drive home the idea of greed as a motivation.

Whether your game is silly or serious, it will make some sort of statement about evil. That statement can be either simple or complex. *The Bloody Inn* makes a fairly simple statement: that greed is the root of greater acts of evil. I try to make a more complicated statement in *Deadly Dowagers*: strong ambition in a repressive society can lead to evil acts. I rely on both internal and external sources of motivation to justify character actions. The theme relies on players having a passing familiarity with the role of women in the Victorian era. Internally, the mechanics show that repressiveness as well as showing the single-minded pursuit of gain by distilling otherwise thematically named actions, such as the "cause of death" cards, to monetary transactions.[17] Unlike *The Bloody Inn*, *Deadly Dowagers* tries to (partially) avoid absurdity by portraying a more complex motivation.

Playable characters require more justification for their actions than non-playable characters, because of how the player relates to their avatar. Asking players to perform actions that represent evil acts should not be a decision you make lightly. Believable villain avatars need context, motivation, abstraction, and an intentional message about the nature of evil in order to be effective. Absurdity is optional but helps draw players in. Should you design evil avatars in board games? If you are interested in experience-driven design and thoughtful thematic integration, evil avatars can pack a punch. If you are only interested in evil avatars because they sound cool, I wouldn't recommend them to you.

Exercise 7.1: Pick one of your designs or a published game that has characters with statistics. List out the characters' goals, values, and feelings about the culture they live in based on their mechanical presentation. Do these traits resemble how they are presented thematically?

Exercise 7.2: Take the list of character traits from the previous exercise and shuffle them so that the characters now have different goals. How would this change their statistics? Does this make the characters more interesting or more nonsensical?

Exercise 7.3: Pick one of your designs or a published thematic game. How does the theme create motivation? What mechanics support that motivation? What could the designer have done differently to strengthen the motivations in the game?

Exercise 7.4: Pick a game with a villain character. What makes them a villain mechanically? What statement does the theme make about villainy?

NOTES

1. Board games are, after all, largely about choices.
2. You can write in the lore that your character likes ice cream, but if ice cream isn't relevant to gameplay, your character's desire for it doesn't do much to create a sense of who they are within the game world.
3. The next section of this chapter discusses categories of character motivation which can deepen player experience.

4. *Player's Handbook*. Renton, WA: Wizards of the Coast, 2014: 125–141.
5. I would prefer that the background section should have one big trait table for all the backgrounds to give a more interesting selection.
6. I explore this topic on my blog where I rely heavily on *Emotional Design* by Donald Norman. (New York: Basic Books, 2004).
7. Resonance is explored more in Chapter 11.
8. Steven Reiss and Susan M. Havercamp, "Toward a comprehensive assessment of fundamental motivation: Factor structure of the Reiss Profiles." *Psychological Assessment, 10*(2), (1998): 97–106. doi:10.1037/1040-3590.10.2.97.
9. Abraham H. Maslow. "A theory of human motivation." *Psychological Review, 50*(4), (1943): 370–396. doi: 10.1037/h0054346.
10. In board games. I'm not looking at representation across all media.
11. Which is to say that differences in politics, including warlike actions, are not inherently evil within the definition I am using here. I am making this distinction because many gamers avoid games that portray a specific or historical evil but don't flinch at games that portray abstracted evils, such as ahistorical or fictional warmongering.
12. Although I think you should try.
13. Any small-ish card game will be necessarily abstracted because cards have inherently abstract qualities to them.
14. Abstraction is discussed more in Chapter 10.
15. Much of the positive feedback for this game was how well the theme came through a euro-style game. But I feel that is a failing of other euros, not a saving grace of *Abomination*.
16. Games are about choices, so themes that remove characters' free will have an inherent conflict between player and avatar if not addressed with a certain amount of nuance within the theme.
17. Reducing murder to a profit generating mechanism could be bad design if it were unintentional. But I intentionally crafted some thematic dissonance into the game as a part of the experience. Intentionality does not absolve you of unfortunate thematic implications, but can help lead a design to more interesting places.

REFERENCES

1. *Player's Handbook*. Renton, WA: Wizards of the Coast, 2014.
2. Norman, Donald. Emotional Design. New York: Basic Books, 2004.
3. Reiss, Steven and Susan M. Havercamp. "Toward a comprehensive assessment of fundamental motivation: Factor structure of the Reiss Profiles." *Psychological Assessment, 10*(2), (1998): 97–106. doi: 10.1037/1040-3590.10.2.97.
4. Maslow, Abraham H. "A theory of human motivation." Psychological Review, *50*(4), (1943): 370–396. doi: 10.1037/h0054346.

GAMES REFERENCED

Deadly Dowagers
Root
Agricola
Dungeons and Dragons
Ex Libris
Deep Sea Adventure
The Bloody Inn
Abomination: Heir of Frankenstein
Sheriff of Nottingham

CHAPTER 8

Setting

MODES OF SETTING EXPRESSION

In the previous three chapters, I have outlined ways of looking at plot and character in board game design. This chapter is all about setting. Remember that in board game parlance, theme encompasses both subject—characters performing actions—and setting—the context for the actions.

Integrating the setting of your game into the mechanics is harder than integrating plot and character. There is a lot more nuance and artistry involved. Real-world settings require research and cultural consultants.[1] In real or fictional themes, setting done well will add texture and depth of experience. Relying solely on illustration and narrative text for setting ignores a number of tools that can add richness to your theme.

Setting is often expressed solely through illustration, which makes it very easy to change the setting during development or for later editions. However, there are a number of ways setting can be expressed more deeply in a game. The following concepts are all aspects of setting that can be represented in a game design: geographic location, laws of physics, passage of time, history of location, local laws and politics, cultural mores, emotional atmosphere of narrative, genre tropes outside of the plot, and any other forms of context that inform the narrative.

Before we jump into mechanical expression of theme, consider how components are typically used to express theme. Boards are large and static as far as components go, which is why they are effective at representing locations. The action of the game is done on the board, within the

DOI: 10.1201/9781003453765-10

location. Tiles are used for locations that are undergoing drastic change during the course of the game or to simulate travel to unknown locations.[2] Cards and tokens are often used to represent people and items—things that can move or be moved around a location. Dice are generally abstract, which makes them well-suited to representing non-physical elements such as actions. This isn't prescriptive; feel free to explore other thematic uses for components. The point is that designers should take advantage of the types of information components are better suited to convey.

Consideration for how components can express the characteristics of what they represent is important in a well-knitted theme. Using components to reinforce the rules of the game world grounds the game in its setting. Using components in ways that are unintuitive can unmoor a game from its setting. In Chapter 4, we looked at the component differences between *Sushi Go!* and *Sushi Roll*. *Sushi Go!* uses cards to represent sushi and *Sushi Roll* uses dice. Both use their components in an intuitive manner to represent collecting sushi. If the sushi was represented by areas of a board that players collected by placing cubes in different areas, that use of mechanics would be unintuitive to the theme.

When we talk about user experience (or UX) in game design, we usually talk about the importance of affordances. Affordances are the qualities of objects that signal to the user how the object is meant to be used. Components have some intrinsic affordances. The fact that cards are meant to be held in a hand and tiles usually are not is intuitive to the user because one is more comfortable to hold for several minutes than the other. We can also provide thematic affordances to our players. An example of a thematic affordance could be segments of roads needing to connect to already placed roads. People generally do not drive into an open field and start building a road from the middle. Using thematic affordances to represent real-world constraints is an expression of a realistic setting, discussed below. Real-world analogs are the easiest, most effective way to use thematic affordances, but you can also make use of genre tropes or a player's knowledge of the IP that the game is based on. The conveyor belt boards of *Sushi Roll* that transport the dice around the table have better affordances than the cards of *Sushi Go!*. As a result, the rules are more intuitive. Because the affordances are representative of the setting, the theme is more effectively expressed.

Setting can be expressed in a realistic way, a stylized way, or an associated way. Realistic setting does the most to reinforce worldbuilding.

Settings expressed in a realistic style can use simulative actions, metaphoric actions, and literal actions to enhance the sense of location.[3] Elements of setting can be presented as simulations or metaphors through the use of rules to provide similar boundaries and affordances found in their real-world counterparts. For example, moving vehicle pawns down a road drawn on a board would be a simulative action. *Sushi Roll* uses simulative actions, whereas *Sushi Go!* trends toward metaphorical actions. The next section, Purposes of Setting, breaks various representations of setting into four broad categories. Realistic settings will largely be found in the first two categories: physical place and anthropology. Note that realistic settings are grounded in real-world logic and physics but do not have to be totally free from imaginary elements. Alternate history, horror, and hard science fiction are all literary genres that can take place in realistic settings.

Stylized setting does not map onto real-world concepts, but instead breaks from reality to achieve a certain effect. Settings do not have to be merely realistic representations of the physical or cultural traits of locations. Settings can be stylized for emotional effect, even if the overall depiction is largely grounded in real-world logic. For example, the gameplay of *Root* is based on counter-insurgency or COIN games, which fall into the war game genre. However, by setting the game in a world of cute animals, *Root* creates a less desperate and violent atmosphere. This more welcoming and gentle atmosphere is largely responsible for the game's popularity, because people who don't like war games were willing to try it.

Stylized settings may be so far from reality that they dispense with real-world logic entirely. For example, *Cosmic Frog* uses very little in the way of real-world affordances. The mechanics of the game are largely tile collection and battling other players. Here is the setting of *Cosmic Frog*:

> *Cosmic Frog* is a game of collection, combat, and theft on a planetary scale. Each player controls a two-mile-tall, immortal, invulnerable frog-like creature that exists solely to gather terrain from the Shards of Aeth, the fragments of a long-ago shattered world. The First Ones seek to use the lands from the Shards to reconstruct the world of Aeth, and your frogs are their terrain harvesters.[4]

The gameplay of *Cosmic Frog* maps more closely to the video game *Super Smash Bros.* than it does anything in the real world. The setting of mythological, world-eating frogs signals to the player that they shouldn't expect the gameplay to follow real-world logic. This expectation is reinforced by the art in the game.

The stylized setting of *Cosmic Frog* is an example of fantasy. Fantasy in this context is an art term that means images and themes that depict things that could never exist in reality.[5] A fantastical way of presenting roads would be to ignore distances in favor of portals that move pawns instantly from one point to another. Obviously, some game mechanics will have that type of point-to-point movement even if the setting is a realistic one that includes illustrations of roads. This is a case where understanding how theme can be expressed helps you make decisions in what your rules represent. If a theme is realistic but all the mechanics lean more into fantasy logic, the game will feel more abstract and disconnected from the theme. If you include one or two simulative mechanics, the theme will feel more grounded in reality. If you pair fantastical mechanics with a stylized setting, you still need to make sure that the theme provides affordances for the player. In *Cosmic Frog*, the frogs can jump and swallow, which maps on to our basic understanding of frogs. The fact that these frogs are jumping on and swallowing pieces of a broken world doesn't impede our understanding of how these actions work. If the avatars were more generic fantasy monsters, players would have fewer affordances to help them remember how actions work.

Another form of stylized presentation is hierarchic scaling, which presents more important information in a larger format. In our road example, roads that are more frequently traveled would be drawn to be larger. *The Pillars of the Earth* popularized the idea of a larger worker piece that is able to take a more powerful version of an action.[6] Hierarchic scaling is almost always metaphoric rather than simulative, although it could be simulative if the illustration indicated that some characters were simply taller and stronger than others. Rather, component size is used to indicate that there is something special about the large worker. This may seem more like a function of UI than setting. I mention hierarchic scaling here because it is a principle of stylized art and to point out that stylized themes and game elements can serve practical functions beyond creating atmosphere. It is also an example of stylized elements that are frequently used in realistic settings.

Of course, many settings are a combination of realistic and stylized. Most fantasy themes combine real-world logic, like geography or gravity, with magic. *Root* is more realistic than stylized, but it uses the combination of modes to great effect. Realistic elements provide logical justifications for rules. When your rules make perfect sense within your theme, players learn them quicker. Logical elements can make complex game systems more accessible. Some stylized elements increase rules accessibility, like hierarchic scaling, but others may not.

Lastly, associated setting will feel layered rather than knitted. Associated mechanics are ones that are merely labeled thematically but are totally abstracted. Tracks are a common associated mechanic. Associated settings are settings that are depicted in the illustration and lore but feel disconnected from gameplay. If the setting has no impact on gameplay, you may want to ask yourself if there is a setting that would better support the experience of play or if there is a way to mechanically express the setting. While I concede that associated mechanics are often necessary (you can't simulate everything), I strongly dislike associated settings. To me, it says that the publisher wants me to buy the game because I like the art, not because the art is connected to the experience of play in any way. I like abstract games. If I play a thematic game, I want the theme to be incorporated into the game.

Which style of setting you use depends on what affordances you want your rules and mechanics to convey. Do you want to convey a world grounded in recognizable logic and physics? Do you want to convey a dreamscape? Something in between? The internal logic of your setting is dictated by how you theme your game elements.

PURPOSES OF SETTING

Realistic setting and stylized setting are (for the most part) stylistic choices of how you present your setting/theme. The choice of realistic or stylized for a thematic element comes down to the type of logic you wish to present through that element. Most thematic games will have a combination of realistic and stylized elements. How all those elements come together will determine whether the game feels more realistic or stylized as a whole.

However, we can and should get a lot more detailed when thinking about setting. Our designs can contain a lot of theme outside of characters, their goals, and their obstacles. It is all of these other elements that create the context that the characters operate within. Setting is a very broad term that can be broken down into a few more specific categories. Which types of setting you use depend on what you are trying to evoke in your design. Not every game needs every possible expression of setting, but hopefully thinking about setting in a variety of ways will help you to come up with better-knitted thematic solutions during the design process.

Setting as a Physical Place

When you use realistic elements to evoke a physical place, you are signaling that your theme is grounded in real-world logic and physics. Even if the world is a fantasy world, you can use game elements to evoke comprehensible concepts to the players. There should be a logic to why the world works the way it does and that logic should (at least partly) be evident to the players. If you are trying to evoke a sense of place, that means you should have an idea of what that place is like.

Geographic location can be shown via maps and illustration or through the types of actions and resources available. A house will be illustrated differently than a mountain but will also provide a different environment for players to interact with. A necessary resource might not be found in the location where the game takes place. One way to show that would be to have that resource only available through purchase rather than collection. This simple mechanism provides a sense of locality to certain resources, a sense of economic trade within the society, and a sense that this location does not exist in isolation within the world. It does not take much to evoke a setting.

Different locations will also have different accumulations of natural phenomena. While laws of physics don't change, natural phenomena, such as weather patterns, will vary in frequency in different locations. Game designs may seek to capture temperature, precipitation, natural disasters, gravity, air current/wind, biome growth, natural selection, etc. in their mechanisms. The cooperative card game *The Coldest Night* models severe cold through negative effect cards, and most of the game focuses on building a fire without smothering it. The focus on maintaining heat to avoid frostbite strongly evokes the setting and provides an easily accessible motivation to players. Everyone has been cold before and most people have been around an open fire. Natural forces are the expression of setting that should be most familiar to designers, because of the ubiquity of nature-themed games that model some sort of natural process.

Attention to the amount of thematic time elapsed within turns and between turns can make actions feel more grounded in reality. Some actions may take longer to accomplish than others; actions that require more time mechanically could also require more time thematically (and vice versa). The most common example of thematic time in a game is the time track mechanism. Time is a currency that when spent pushes you down a track. Turn order is determined by who is the farthest back on the track. *Tokaido*, a set collection game, couples this concept with that of physical geography so that the track is a road that players move down through time. *The Search for Planet X*, a deduction puzzle game, uses a time track to simulate the amount of time elapsed during astronomical surveys of the night sky. Both games have realistic settings and incorporate time into their realism.

So-called "real time" games use timers instead of a track so that all players take actions simultaneously within the time limit. This can either increase the simulation of the theme or greatly decrease it depending on how it is implemented. Manipulation of sand timers adds a frenetic quality to a game, but is not particularly thematic. Using an app, like in *UBOOT: The Board Game*, can add to the simulation by having the timer "off screen." *UBOOT* is a cooperative, real-time game themed around submarine warfare that uses an app to manage both the timer and hidden information. The simulation feels more real because players do not have to interact with the timer. The app also adds to the experience through the sound effects it uses during the timed portion of play.

Setting as Anthropology

Real-world logic extends not just to a location, but also to the people who live there. If your theme includes sentient life, you'll want to consider the impact that life has on your world. Settings that contain intelligent life forms will be impacted by those life forms even if they are not represented in the game. *Petrichor* has players controlling clouds whose stated purpose is to water crops, specifically, as opposed to plants more generally. The existence of crops (and, in an expansion, cows) provides a setting where human farmers are active participants in the life cycle, even if they are not depicted in the game.

Where intelligent life has an impact on setting, there are a number of ways that can be represented. History, like geography, can permeate illustrations as well as mechanisms. On the illustration side, shiny new buildings deliver a different concept of history than ruins do. On the mechanism side, knowing your setting's history can help tailor the rules to give a better sense of why things work the way they do in this setting.

Games with combat especially benefit from having a sense of why the conflict exists, of what is worth dying for. Local laws or politics also add justification for certain rules, but in turn can add immersion by implying there are in-world lawmakers behind the rules. Even if you are playing as the lawmakers, older laws or traditions could impose restrictions on how you must act. Cultural mores are social guidelines that are enforced by a particular culture. Cultural mores could include religious practices, acceptable dress, food taboos, good manners, etc. Traditions are one aspect of cultural mores. Many laws are universal across cultures, such as prohibition of stealing, but cultural mores are distinct to a specific culture. Representing cultural mores or values in some way helps your setting feel like it belongs to a specific culture instead of using that culture as window dressing. Recall that in Chapter 7 we looked at how factions are the result of conflicting cultural values. Lastly, technology does not spring from a vacuum, but is informed by the history, laws, and mores of a society.

This sounds a lot more complicated than it is. You do not have to do very much to convey a sense of society. In Chapter 7, I mentioned *Root* as an example of mechanics showing the culture of the game world. *Root* uses lengthy asymmetric rules to show the history and politics of its world. Many games make do with less. *Star Realms* is a game consisting of 128 cards. The game world consists of four factions vying for power. The designers only had 20 cards per faction to express the values and technological capabilities present in the game world alongside compelling mechanics. Furthermore, the values of the factions are represented almost purely by the mechanics with a slight assist from the illustration. The factions are not only mechanically distinct, but the mechanics show the technological and societal differences between the factions in a way that is intuitive. Simply making one faction more defensive and focused on income says a lot about the values of that faction. Naming that faction the Trade Federation functions to help the player remember what the faction is good at. The mechanics of the other factions hint at the technology in the world. The alien Blobs have stronger attacks when alongside other Blob ships, hinting at their techno-biological construction. The Machine Cult focuses on scrapping ships, that is removing undesirable cards from your deck. The most direct way to give players a glimpse into the game world is to design a faction or character that is good at something and have what they are good at be important both to them and the world they exist in.

Setting as Atmosphere

Atmosphere is the mood or tone conveyed by a setting. Color choice and line quality are aspects of illustration that convey atmosphere. Being able to communicate what kind of atmosphere your setting has is important even if you aren't a visual artist. For example, you may need to give guidelines to an illustrator that the art should have muted colors and flowing lines, or dark, saturated colors and sharp, abrupt lines. Those instructions leave plenty of room for the creativity of the illustrator, but they each convey very different atmospheres. Atmosphere is also conveyed through gameplay. The relative intensity of gameplay creates an atmosphere for the game that will either work with or against your setting. Tight and tense mechanics provide a different experience than cozy and breezy mechanics. The setting can reinforce the experience of the mechanics; it can mitigate that experience; it can provide commentary on the type of experience provided by the mechanics (see below); or it can feel mismatched and lead to player dissatisfaction. *Root* is an example of a setting of cute woodland creatures mitigating the experience of a high conflict game.

Time, as an experiential element as opposed to a realistic simulation, can be used to give a sense of urgency or calm: the pace of the gameplay is a major component of a game's emotional atmosphere. A push your luck game treats time differently than a civilization game. Downtime between turns makes more sense in a theme where you don't feel pressed for time. How cozy or intense a game feels is largely due to how a game manages a player's time.

Genre tropes can provide shortcuts to conveying atmosphere through illustration or thematic labeling of actions and resources. Genre tropes are common conventions that get recycled so often in media that they can become hallmarks of a genre, such as the final girl in horror movies. By presenting familiar tropes, you provide players with clues for what to expect from the experience of play. Thematic genres include horror, old west, pirates, fantasy, scifi, etc. When you set your game in a familiar genre, you create expectations that the game will provide a certain experience. You must either fulfill those expectations or subvert them in a satisfying way.

Setting as Commentary

Setting can never be totally divorced from the cultural context of the audience that is consuming the media. Setting a game in a particular time and place will convey meaning to players, often in the form of subtext. *The Grizzled* is a cooperative card game where players assume the role of soldiers in WWI. The game focuses not on winning battles but surviving them. *The Grizzled* works as a commentary on war because it is set in a particularly horrific war that is also far enough removed in history that no one alive today fought in it. The intended audience is also familiar enough with WWI that they can jump right in with limited explanation of the setting. The commentary is fairly surface level (war is more tragic than glorious), thus not risking misinterpretation.

In other media, settings can be metaphors used to comment on contemporary issues. Board games are only beginning to explore satire and commentary, and I am unaware of a published game that makes a point about something different from what the game purports to be about.[7] I anticipate that over time board games will expand more into the territory of intentional commentary. I wouldn't recommend new designers start at this point. However, it is important to acknowledge that the hobby is filled with games that are unintentional commentaries on which perspectives they elevate and which they ignore.

Rules can convey physics—movement, speed, gravity, etc.—via simulative mechanics. Rules can convey societal values via simulative or stylized mechanics. Historical laws can be represented by simulative mechanics, but social mores could be evoked through mechanics that provide the same emotional feeling as living in the society depicted. Societal values can be conveyed through how open or restrictive the rules are, whether the game is cooperative or competitive, which resources are the most expensive, and what goals the game presents to the players.

In addition to story structure aligning with game structure, we also must give our settings enough touchstones to provide a sense of place: geographical, anthropological, atmospheric, or metaphoric. While it sounds like a lot of work, really what you will be doing is imagining the world you are trying to evoke and limiting some of your design decisions to options that best evoke that world. That's really what design is: imagining possibilities, curating ideas, and implementing the best ideas into the whole project.

Exercise 8.1: Pick one of your designs or a published game. What is the setting? Is the setting expressed realistically, artistically, or in some other way? What changes would make the setting more clearly expressed?

Exercise 8.2: Pick one of your designs or a published game. What categories of setting are present: physical place, laws of physics, history, politics, culture, atmosphere, genre tropes? How do these elements inform the mechanics?

NOTES

1. Fictional themes may also require cultural consultants.
2. Sometimes cards are used as tiles.
3. Action types are discussed in Chapter 2.
4. Devious Weasel Games, "Cosmic Frog," *Board Game Geek*, August 5, 2020. https://boardgamegeek.com/boardgame/295905/cosmic-frog.
5. Fantasy is discussed more in Chapter 11.
6. This mechanism is sometimes called a grande worker, which is a term taken from the game *Viticulture*.
7. The play *The Crucible*, for instance, is set during the Salem witch trials but is a commentary on McCarthyism.

REFERENCE

1. Devious Weasel Games. "Cosmic Frog." Board Game Geek. August 5, 2020. https://boardgamegeek.com/boardgame/295905/cosmic-frog.

GAMES REFERENCED

Sushi Go!
Sushi Roll
Root
Cosmic Frog
The Pillars of the Earth
The Coldest Night
Tokaido
The Search for Planet X
UBOOT: The Board Game
Petrichor
Star Realms
The Grizzled

CHAPTER 9

Putting It All Together

LET'S PUT TOGETHER WHAT we've covered so far in two different ways. First, let's take a look at how all of these terms apply to a simple, thematic game. Then, I have created a design "cheat sheet" to reference when you are building your theme.

APPLYING CHAPTERS 1–8

Sushi Go! is an affordable and easy to learn set collection game.[1] *Sushi Go!* is not a narrative game. You may read this book and feel that this game fails on a number of levels thematically. However, not all games need to express theme using all the principles described in this book. Instead, having read this far in this book you can now express the exact level of theme present in *Sushi Go!*.

From Chapter 1, we know that a theme is a subject in a setting with an uncertain outcome. The theme of *Sushi Go!* is customers in a restaurant selecting sushi for their meal. The subject is customers selecting sushi. The setting is a sushi restaurant. The uncertain outcome is the exact meals the customers will have and who will have the best meal.

Chapter 2 looked at two types of integration between theme and mechanisms—layering and knitting—and different types of thematic actions. The theme in *Sushi Go!* is loosely knitted to the mechanics. The card drafting mechanism is a metaphoric action that borders on simulative,[2] but the set collection scoring is mostly mechanical. The chopsticks card, which allows you to pick up two pieces of sushi, and the wasabi card also border on simulative. Wasabi is the most simulative action in the game because

DOI: 10.1201/9781003453765-11

you must place the card down and then physically place another sushi card on top of it to score.

Chapter 3 looked at two styles of game structure: metaphors that mechanisms can be built around and mechanical structures that theme can be built around. The central metaphor in *Sushi Go!* is the drafting mechanism that represents a conveyor belt of sushi. The game is cyclical in structure; there are three rounds in which players repeat the same actions.

Chapter 4 looked at building theme around goals and obstacles, converting goals to mechanical actions, and how to manage the non-thematic aspects of a game. The goal of *Sushi Go!* is for the customer to have the best meal, and the obstacle is that other customers are also taking sushi as it passes by. The player actions are entirely acquisitive with an automatic deployment action of laying the acquired cards into a tableau, which fits with the theme of collecting sushi on a plate. Drawing cards at the start of each round and scoring are purely game state and do not affect the game world. There are two pauses between the rounds of drafting, in addition to the interruptions to game flow that can be caused by a player's analysis paralysis when selecting which card to draft.

Chapter 5 looked at narrative framing and story structure for non-narrative games. *Sushi Go!* is framed around customers in a restaurant having a meal. Because the theme and narrative are so simple, the narrative framing becomes a restatement of the theme. The scope of the theme is a narrow focus of one meal at a restaurant. The resolution of the theme is somewhat low, especially compared to the more simulative *Sushi Roll. Sushi Go!* does not depict conveyor belts or plates or menus or prices. Despite the three rounds of the game, the story structure contains only a single scene, albeit one that involves three plates of food. There is no particular inciting incident, exposition, or denouement.

Chapter 6 looked at various ways that players interface with their characters. In *Sushi Go!*, players are self-insert characters and occupy the role of the hero. Player strategies include the positive optimization of trying to efficiently get the most points across three rounds which feels thematic, but also the unthematic strategies of denial and "cut your losses."

Chapter 7 looked at ways to make characters more narratively interesting in non-narrative games. In *Sushi Go!*, the characters' goals do align with the win condition of having the best meal. The characters do not have unique abilities, which indicates that all the characters are striving to have a good meal for similar reasons. The rules do reflect the norms and etiquette of a conveyor belt sushi restaurant by preventing a player from simply grabbing all the sushi at once. We are not told why the customers want to have the best meal (or even eat that much sushi), but we can assign the universal need to eat and desire to collect as driving motivations for the characters.

Chapter 8 looked at styles and types of setting. The setting of *Sushi Go!* is associated with a physical place, but we don't get much of a sense of the restaurant beyond the appearance of the sushi. The logic of the mechanics is realistic, even though it is not detailed.

Is much of this expression of theme lost on the players? Yes. The same way most viewers of a Renaissance painting will fail to see how the painter used the finer points of art theory to create the painting. Nevertheless, these elements of theory add up to a positive end user experience in both cases.

THEME-BUILDING QUICK GUIDE

What follows is a thematic design "cheat sheet." I have combined ideas from the previous chapters and simplified them into a few points that you should consider when theme-building.

Story and Gameplay: What is the Action of the Game?

The story of a game is not the lore you write at the beginning of the rulebook. The story is the events that happen to the characters during gameplay. The story begins either during setup or on the first turn and ends either on the last turn or during scoring. That is the whole extent of the lives of the characters that players are witness to. Good worldbuilding does not require extra lore. We can learn a lot about a world just by playing a game. In game design, actions speak louder than words. Any lore you write about the characters needs to feel as though it could come from the same world as what is experienced during gameplay.

Most hobby games these days are designed with some theme in mind. Also, many mechanics have inherent themes, such as worker placement or pick-up-and-deliver. No matter where your game is set in space and time, pick-up-and-deliver mechanics will broadly convey similar themes. When focusing on worldbuilding, we can adjust our mechanics to better express our themes, and we can develop our themes to better fit our mechanics.

Do your mechanics tell the story of your theme?

Goals and Win Conditions: What is at Stake?

Characters need thematic goals, and those goals should closely align to the win condition of the game. Thematic goals will be assumed to align with characters' desires. Oftentimes, all characters will share the same goal. However, if win conditions vary by character, that means their thematic goals do as well. A character trying to build an engine has different goals than a character trying to dismantle an engine. When a character's goal is closely tied to the player's goal, the mechanics become more immersive for the player.

Does your win condition align with your characters' goals and desires?

Roles and Utility: How Does a Character Fit into the Game World?

A character's role in the game should map to their role in the world. In other words, a character's title or job description should look like what they do mechanically. A soldier is useful in combat; a mechanic fixes things; etc. What actions do your mechanics represent and what job would encompass those actions? Sometimes more than one role would work to represent a given action. A helicopter pilot can move to any location, but so can a UN ambassador. Which job title you choose depends on your own knowledge of your game world. You shouldn't call your character "The Flirt" if that characteristic is not present in their mechanics. Since a game is a relatively small window into a world, a role will usually feel like a character's purpose in life.

Do your characters' roles fit with both the actions they take and the story of the game?

World Views and Powers/Skills: What Does a Character Value?

Characters' special powers or skills represent their world view—what they are willing to do to achieve their goals. Characters' world views may be in conflict with other characters, even if they share the same goal. A character who kills to achieve their goal has a different perspective and set of values than a character who negotiates. In a competitive game, competing values between characters drives the narrative conflict behind why the characters are in competition. In a cooperative game, the tension of conflicting world views could help create drama and encourage role playing, or it could make the game less immersive, depending on how that tension is handled. Addressing why a character behaves the way they do can lead to immersion, but isn't necessary for every game. If your characters are unnamed job titles, you may not want to worry about their personal values. However, most people take jobs that fit their value system, unless they are driven to other work through necessity.

If you have a design in development that does not have a theme or needs to be rethemed, try to identify any personality or values conveyed by the mechanics. How do the characters move? Violently? Gracefully? Stealthily? Does a character rely on strength? How would physical traits translate into personality traits? Much of the time, personality traits are only expressed in the illustrations. However, knowing what your characters value and how they achieve goals is important while you are playtesting and changing mechanisms. When you are faced with multiple valid paths for development, knowing who your characters are can help narrow down which path is the right one.

Knowing who your characters are also helps when coming up with special powers. I can play a perfectly balanced, asymmetrical game and still feel like there was nothing unique about the characters. This is most often the case when the mechanics do not evoke the theme enough. In this case, try changing how those mechanics are themed. If a mechanic still does not feel thematic, I would look at changing it to better suit my character. Some mechanics, like scoring, will very rarely feel thematic and that's ok. Pay the most attention to the mechanics that happen on the board (or in the tableau, etc.). The board represents the game world, so the mechanics around it need to feel the most thematic.

Do your characters' skills in your game express their values?

Factions and Politics: What is the Root of the Conflict?

Characters are not always unique individuals. Sometimes they are factions or groups. How factions relate to one another usually indicates the political landscape of the game world. Factions form when two or more groups have conflicting values and goals. You should know why your factions want to kill each other and what each side stands to gain if they win.

Why does each side want to win in your game?

Your mechanics will tell a story during gameplay. Your theme and mechanics should be telling similar stories. Give extra attention to win conditions and special powers, because those mechanisms convey a lot of story details. Knowing who your character is means knowing how they feel about the other characters. Characters can have more complex relationships than merely on-my-team and enemy-I-try-to-kill.

Exercise 9.1: Return to the theme from Exercise 1.1. Without looking at your previous answer, list the subject, setting, and how they connect with the mechanics. Has your answer changed?

NOTES

1. If you can't get a physical copy to play, there are playthroughs you can watch online.
2. I would argue that *Sushi Roll*'s conveyor tiles are simulative, and that *Sushi Go*! never rises to that level of modeling.

GAMES REFERENCED

Sushi Go!

THREE

Thematic Design Process

CHAPTER 10

Ideas and Research

HOW TO HAVE GOOD IDEAS

The previous two sections of this book have discussed what theme is, how it is expressed, and how certain expressions of theme can build game narrative. This section looks at the design process and how theme fits into that process. This chapter looks at the beginning of the process: ideas and research.

Every design starts with an idea. Have you ever been jealous of a game that had a really good concept? Do you ever feel like your ideas just aren't as good as other designers? The good news is, good ideas are more likely the result of iteration, not inspiration. Chances are, your initial inspiration is not a great idea. No idea survives contact with a first playtest. As we develop our designs, they become better ideas. However, "just work on it longer" is not a recipe for having better ideas. It is part of it but not even the biggest part.

The most important step is to develop a habit of curiosity. Be interested in the world around you. Learn about how and why things work the way they do. Read books; watch documentaries; listen to podcasts. Explore anything you find intriguing. Abstracts of scholarly papers are a good place to find succinct information. I have read dissertations that were available for free online. The inspiration for a recent design of mine came from a joke in a TV show that was based on a real holiday tradition. My later research led me to a first-hand account of the tradition as practiced in the nineteenth century. I should note that fiction can be as valuable as non-fiction. However, media that allows for deep dives tends

DOI: 10.1201/9781003453765-13

to work better. Don't just watch a movie; study an entire genre. On the mechanics side, this means playing lots of games.[1] Most importantly, be interested and follow your interests.

This habit over time will build what I think of as an "idea compost heap." Plants more easily spring up from a compost heap that has had a lot of material added and then is allowed to settle. The media you consume is information that can become ideas. The media is not by itself ideas or even research; research is what happens after you have an idea. The information you absorb will settle in your mind. Then, when you start working on new designs, ideas will begin to sprout.

But where do you start, when you begin a design from scratch? I don't think simply saying "start with theme first" or "mechanics first" is particularly useful or descriptive. Most design ideas start as an attempt to answer a question—what would a game about X look like? Asking "what if" is a powerful tool at any point in the design process but perhaps especially at the beginning. Reflecting on the question you are attempting to answer is also an important tool. Ask yourself, "Is this question interesting? Is there another question about this topic that would be more interesting to answer?"

Asking interesting questions leads to more interesting design choices. If a question does not inspire options to explore in your design, it is not an interesting question. "Can I design a quality worker placement game?" is not an interesting question. "What would a worker placement game about a labor revolt look like?" is an interesting question. Good questions are inspiring and lead to improved ideas.

The types of questions you ask may begin from a number of different places: mechanics, theme, components, title of game, intended play experience, etc. Where you begin is not as important as where you end up. An overemphasis on the starting point can lead designers to think that ideas need to start out good, or that the starting point always needs to be in the same place. Ideas are more like gardening than construction. You can prune all you like, but if the idea wants to grow a certain way, you are better off letting it go in the unexpected direction.

Often designs start as a question that combines both theme and mechanics: How can I mechanically represent this real-world concept? What theme would fit with this abstract mechanism? Or questions may combine emotion with mechanics or theme: How can I make a worker placement game feel more tense? How can my design give the experience of riding a roller coaster, instead of mechanically simulating a roller coaster? Interesting questions can lead to ideas around game structure, metaphors, goals, and obstacles. A cyclical game might adequately simulate a theme park ride, but may not provide the intended excitement, unless combined with a race to finish structure.

As your design develops, you will add questions that need to be answered. If your initial question was about theme and mechanics, you will need to ask, "What experience does this combination provide? Is it the kind of experience I want players to have?" Other questions can and should include any topic covered in this book. Are your characters interesting? Is the conflict clear? These are also questions you can pose to your playtesters.

At any stage of design, you should reflect on the questions you are asking and return to the question, "Is this interesting? Does it hold my interest?" If the answer is no, it is time to iterate—to explore different questions. Find new answers and see if any spark ideas that will take the design in new directions. Really good ideas come from iteration.

PURPOSES OF RESEARCH

Once you have an idea, research can help give you a direction for your design. Why research theme? Shouldn't gameplay be prioritized over theme? I usually spend at least several days early in my design process researching theme. My research helps shape my intended core experience which informs how my core loop develops. While researching, I always find ideas that are better than anything I could invent. This section lists four ways research will have a positive impact on your game.

Abstraction

The predominant argument against extensive thematic research is that games are abstractions, and as such, they cannot present very much in the way of thematic detail, especially mechanically—so why bother spending valuable design time researching? However, abstraction from lack of knowledge conveys ideas more poorly than abstraction from knowledge of a subject. Abstraction is the removal of details in order to present a more simplified representation of a concept. Knowing what details to preserve and which to remove requires an understanding of the subject you are abstracting. I prefer *Bang!* to all other social deduction games that I have played in part because it does the best job at evoking the theme, both subject and setting. Yet few people would list *Bang!* if they were asked to list strongly thematic games. The thematic experience is effective but not extensive; the theme works because of the details which are preserved in a fairly simple game. In a thematic game, abstraction is merely low resolution. The details still need to be evocative of the theme. Additionally, if you start with well-researched elements, it will be easier to add more resolution later, such as with expansion content.

Verisimilitude

Verisimilitude is the appearance of reality. Familiarity with your theme enables you to add the small flourishes that make the game feel grounded in something real. Attention to small details will make your game world feel as though there is a fully formed world that exists beyond the constraints of the game. This is especially true for players who have some prior knowledge of a subject. Players may not notice every detail that flows smoothly within a game, but if there is something that sticks out to them as wrong they will fixate on that detail. Keep in mind that a world you invented will most likely still have elements that exist in reality. Some of my favorite fantasy authors have gotten more mileage out of using obscure but real details than made-up ones. Likewise, many science fiction authors are familiar with theoretical technology design in order to present some plausible elements alongside less plausible ones. Verisimilitude can help your setting feel like a real place with real people. Research within genre media can also be important if the familiarity you are evoking is not reality but conventions within fiction. If you want to play into tropes *or* against tropes, you have to know what the tropes are.

Emotional Knowledge

I'm using the term emotional knowledge to mean an understanding of the emotional content of your theme. Emotional content is a term that describes the emotions elicited by a piece of media. When you are familiar with a subject, you can better judge in what light to present it to your intended audience. Understanding the emotional content of a subject requires more than just cursory knowledge. You have to know the subject well enough to understand how knowledgeable players will feel when they play your game. Most people will forgive the details you sacrifice to the abstraction of gameplay as long as the game "feels" like the theme. Playtesting can help reveal the experience a game will provide, but is limited by the demographics and proclivities of your playtesters. Cultural consultants can help, but awareness of pitfalls at the beginning of a project will be useful both to you and any cultural consultants brought in later in the process. Recall as well that abstraction can be used to shift the focus of an action from the impact of the action to the decision point. Abstraction allows you to play with and tune the emotional content of a theme. However, you first must understand the emotions inherent in the content that you are modeling.

Resonance

Resonance will be covered in detail in Chapter 11. However, it is worth underscoring here the impact of research on resonance. Resonance is the combination of familiarity with unexpectedness and subtracting anything superfluous. Verisimilitude is used to create familiarity; abstraction is used to eliminate superfluous elements. That leaves unexpectedness. Research can reveal delightfully true details that will make your game more memorable by their inclusion. For example, I found a list of real Victorian charities to use as flavor text in *Deadly Dowagers*. The names were far funnier than anything I could come up with and felt more appropriate to the setting because they are contemporary to the setting. Instead of using flavor text to display my own cleverness, I creatively curated details to shine a light on the wacky, delightful things that already exist in the world.

When you research, you should research with an eye for design. Learn how the people closest to the subject matter feel about it. Learn enough of the details to know which to leave out and which to leave in. Make sure to leave in some of the most memorable details, even if they only make it into the rulebook as narrative snippets. A small amount of time spent on research will have a large impact on your final product.

Exercise 10.1: Pick an object you are familiar with and draw a simple symbol that could be used to represent that object in a roll and write game, such as a leaf. Now try to draw symbols to represent these terms: gobo, grommet, dibber, fitch, and gaff. (These are all commonly used objects in various specialized fields.)[2] If you are unfamiliar with the terms, your abstracted icon will likely be unrelated to the actual appearance and use of the object.

Exercise 10.2: Pick one of your designs. Spend five minutes googling an alternative resource for the game. This could be a different form of currency, crop, mineral, or technology. Or pick a generic resource and research a more specific version: barely instead of grain, linen instead of cloth, etc. Does the alternate resource change how you perceive the setting?

Exercise 10.3: Pick a game based on a subject you are familiar with (such as a movie property). Does that game capture the spirit of the subject? In what ways does it succeed? In what ways does it fall short?

Exercise 10.4: Pick one of your designs. Tell the story of the game theme to someone else. Include any interesting details about actions or resources. Ask your listener what they connect with the most and if anything feels missing from the story.

NOTES

1. Or watching videos of actual play. I'm not sure it matters which you do.
2. Gobo: a thin metal disc with a pattern cut out that light shines through, used in theatre to create lighting effects. Grommet: a two-part metal ring clamped to fabric used mostly on curtains. Dibber: a garden planting tool. Fitch: a type of paint brush head. Gaff: a fabric tape reminiscent of duct tape but better.

GAMES REFERENCED

Bang!
Deadly Dowagers

CHAPTER 11

Editing for Resonance

FAMILIARITY AND UNEXPECTEDNESS

As your game develops, your theme will likely need to be refined to better resonate with players. As stated in the previous chapter, resonance is the combination of familiarity with unexpectedness and subtracting anything superfluous. Or more concisely, *resonance is familiarity plus unexpectedness minus chaff.*[1] Familiarity is a concept that should seem obvious but has a lot going on with it. Familiarity is best described by "of course" moments. Of course, wheat makes bread (or flour or animal feed). Of course, the ground floor must be built before the second floor. The more your audience already knows, the less you have to teach them, which makes rules intuitive. Familiarity taps into "show don't tell," which is the major axiom of storytelling. You don't have to explain that two factions hate each other if the emotion comes through in your game. Just because you state something in your lore doesn't mean that the gameplay will support that story. You have to show players what the world is like through your gameplay. Much of what has been discussed in Chapters 4–8 is aimed at creating a sense of familiarity in players through story elements.

Adding familiarity decreases the mental load of the rules, allowing players to internalize rules complexity more easily. If your goal is to increase resolution, as discussed in Chapter 5, adding familiarity may help balance out the increase in complexity that comes with increased resolution. To increase ease of play, familiar elements should be knitted into the design. Evocative actions (metaphoric, simulative, and literal) are the most effective ways to add familiarity in order to decrease mental load.[2]

DOI: 10.1201/9781003453765-14

Familiarity is not enough to make a game stand out in an increasingly crowded market. Unexpectedness adds spice to familiarity. Unexpected elements grab attention and generate interest through breaks in a pattern. However, this requires that you establish a pattern before you disrupt it. If everything is unexpected, then nothing will stand out.

Unexpected thematic elements could be a major aspect of the theme, such as the main characters and their goals, but they do not have to be. They can be small touches that add a sense of surprise to otherwise familiar settings.

Unexpectedness can occur thematically as "whimsy" or fantastical elements that depart from reality. In art design language, fantasy means images and themes that depict things that could never exist in reality—more along the lines of the flying whales from Fantasia 2000 rather than medieval wizards in castles.[3] Whimsy is the inclusion of fantasy elements with a lighter touch. For example, the board game *Four Gardens*, which has a three-dimensional, rotating cardboard tower of resources, is whimsical and creates the unexpectedness needed for resonance. Sometimes, story elements need an extra twist to draw players in. *Caverna* took the general shape of *Agricola* and added cave-dwelling dwarves to the existing farming formula. Neither mining nor farming is unexpected in board games. However, building a farmhouse in a mine is the right amount of unexpectedness to add resonance, even a decade after the game has been released.

Often, the surprising elements will come from research.[4] If your research does not turn up interesting ideas and you are having trouble coming up with a story twist on your own, try using reversals. Reversals take familiar storylines and flip the script. Look at the different story elements of your game, and one at a time imagine they were reversed. Perhaps making the king a queen adds interesting plot implications, but it may only be an art change. If reversing an element makes the story instantly more interesting, that is the direction you should pursue. This is a simple "unexpectedness hack," but not everything is made better by using a reversal. The story you tell still needs to feel motivated by the actions in the game and needs to create the intended emotional responses in players. One of the most common uses of reversals is trope subversion. Trope subversion is when genre media sets up the expectation that a story will play out following the standard conventions and then surprises the audience by going against the expectations. Trope subversion doesn't have to be a complete reversal necessarily. Subverting expectations is a powerful storytelling method and resonance generator. Reversals or subversions can create feelings of imbalance in players that can draw them into a game emotionally because they no longer know exactly what to expect. In Chapter 6, I discussed thinking sideways, which functions as trope subversion.

You can have unexpectedness not just purely in the theme, but in how the theme connects to the mechanics and components. Unexpectedness relating to mechanics or components may be perceived as innovation.[5] Innovation or other forms of uniqueness in gameplay will usually create excitement, but there is a limit to how far uniqueness can take you. Uniqueness is difficult to set as a design goal. While it can be great to stumble into genuine innovation, high quality iteration is easier to plan for and achieve. Also, by making a really resonant game, you can make a game that feels innovative even if every concept is a rehash of something else.

Adding unexpectedness requires interrogating your design. Ask interesting questions of your design. What component would most help drive home the theme? What would make players care more about the characters or story in the game? How can I subvert expectations? I particularly like trope subversion because it requires a minimal amount of effort to achieve unexpectedness. And theme-forward techniques like reversals don't increase the cost of the game the way adding miniatures does. Asking questions of your design requires that you engage with your theme. Don't expect your audience to do imaginative work that you were unwilling to do. Critically examine your theme to see where engagement or interest could be added. Engage your theme and interrogate it. Unexpected elements should still feel as though they belong in the world of the theme.

REMOVING CHAFF

When you know what your theme is—its emotions, plot, location, rhythm, characters, and twist—cut everything else out. Chaff is all the extra stuff your design does not need. Figure out what the core of the theme is, and get rid of everything else. Try to always leave your players wanting more. That feeling will drive engagement more readily than expansive world-building will. Feel free to write a novel about your world, but don't put it in the game box. However, putting a limit on the amount of detail expressed by your theme is not a license to skimp on research. As discussed in

Chapter 10, good research will inform which details are most necessary and evocative.

Good design is about removing clutter. Every detail of your game should reinforce the core theme. Just because a detail fits into the world doesn't mean it belongs in the game. If you really must add details, I do recommend using illustration as a way to convey details that don't impede gameplay. Including a mechanic or component just because "it's cool" will feel gimmicky because it is a gimmick.

I define a gimmick as anything that brings a sense of novelty and appeal but not much else.[6] A gimmick looks cool, but either isn't functional or impedes usability.[7] A gimmick adds more cost than the value of what is received. Every element should feel necessary to the game experience; anything else is a distraction. Your core theme will create your core emotional experience. Adding extraneous elements dilutes that emotional experience. In other words, too much fluff makes your game less resonant.

But there is a compromise here. Don't forget that flavor text and certain similar thematic details are "opt-in" details. Meaning a player can ignore these details if they choose. Flavor text is usually in a small font at the bottom of a card. I have the choice to read it or not. Components and even card art don't give me the option to opt-out; they're too prominent for my eyes to skip over. That's the reason I get frustrated by the lore at the beginning of rulebooks: I can't tell immediately if it contains important information about the game or not. If you want to include extra detail in your game that only provides flavor, it needs to be the kind of detail that players can choose to opt-in to or not.

Removing chaff is also about finding the right proportion between familiar and unexpected elements. Too much unexpectedness is jarring and will disconnect players from the theme. Too much familiarity only becomes a problem when the details stray from the core theme or if the theme is boring. So, generally speaking, leave unexpectedness to a few surprising twists compared to the rest of the game.

Removing chaff will require adding some amount of abstraction. Tabletop board games require abstraction. Even simulations must choose what it is that they simulate. However, what you choose to abstract informs the story that your game tells.

When learning to design lighting for the stage, designers are taught that the way to make something look brighter is to remove lights, not add them. When every light is on, nothing is emphasized. By turning some lights off, areas can be spotlighted to draw the audience's attention. The non-obvious result is that turning lights off can make a stage appear brighter.

Abstraction works the same way when it comes to thematic expression in board games. If you want to tell a certain story or provide a certain experience within your theme, what you abstract is as important as what you simulate. Too many details often result in a cluttered experience where no clear story emerges. Whereas selective abstraction allows for your intended thematic experience to shine.

An easy way to understand this concept is to compare two similar games: *The Grizzled* and *The Coldest Night*. Both are small, cooperative card games. Both involve playing a card from your hand on your turn to a shared tableau. Both have negative effect cards that can accumulate in front of a player. But the experience evoked by each is very different.

The Grizzled leans into the importance of camaraderie between soldiers in WWI. The cards played into the shared tableau are less important thematically than helping your squad get what they need to stay alive. The well-being of your squad is the thematic goal of the game and succeeding in missions takes a back seat to that goal. *The Grizzled* accomplishes this by abstracting the fighting aspect of the theme away almost entirely and simulating the mental trauma caused by warfare. This design choice creates a play experience where the predominant emotion is empathy for the other people around the table.

The Coldest Night, by contrast, has a stronger focus on the environmental setting of the game. In the game, players are trying to keep a fire burning all night by feeding it fuel scavenged from an abandoned house. The health of your group is still important, but it is secondary to the primary goal of keeping the fire burning. Unlike *The Grizzled*, *The Coldest Night* is set in a single location on a single night. The theme plays with a universal human fear of getting caught in the cold. Thematically, hope is centered around the fire, not fellow players.

Neither game is more correct for what it chose to abstract vs. simulate. *The Grizzled* has more "heads up" gameplay as players discuss who they need to help. *The Coldest Night* is more "heads down" as players agonize over how to play out their hands. *The Grizzled* can pack a stronger emotional punch because the theme emphasizes relationships. However, it can also force players to make unthematic plays in order to win the game. By focusing on a simpler experience, *The Coldest Night* provides a stronger simulation.

Importantly, neither game tries to emphasize both an environmental simulation and an emotional one. We don't know where we are in France in *The Grizzled* or why we are stuck with the other players in *The Coldest Night*. Those details aren't only unnecessary; they would detract from the clean experiences both games currently provide.

Designers often interpret "integrate theme and mechanics" to mean "theme everything." This is a good place to start. However, if certain thematic details get in the way of the intended experience, you can streamline your thematic elements to better fit your vision.

IMPROVING THEMATIC ENGAGEMENT

The Ludology episode "GameTek 213.5—The Incan Gold Experiment" discusses an experiment to see whether players would play the same mechanics differently based on the theme of the game.[8] It is also often referenced as proof that theme fades over multiple plays. However, the experimenters weren't trying to test for theme fade, and don't mention it in their findings. Nevertheless, most of us know by experience that it doesn't take very many plays of a game for us to stop engaging with the theme and instead focus on efficiency.

The question then is: Is this progression away from thematic engagement inevitable? Can this progression be slowed? The typical answer to this question is to add more content. Content, such as narrative text and variable scenario setups, allows players to continually see something new within the game. Keeping a game fresh and exciting seems to keep players engaged with the theme. Narrative content is especially good at this. However, there are many ways to fend off theme fade without adding more material to the game box. This section looks at combating theme fade using methods other than the content-based approach.

I think that there is a trap we could fall into if we try to make every play of a game as surprising and engaging thematically as a first play. The first time you view a piece of art or watch a movie or read a book will be a much different experience than subsequent exposures. The question should not be "how do I replicate this experience infinitely?" but "how do I make subsequent experiences also engaging?" I regularly reread novels; most people rewatch movies. Any given radio station only plays about 20 songs. Clearly humans have a capacity for repeated engagement with content. And if I asked you to name a song that always makes you cry you probably could, showing that we can repeatedly engage with emotional content as well.

What, then, is going on with our disengagement with the theme in board games? I would posit that in the early plays of a game, we are more likely to engage with opt-in thematic elements, and in later plays, we ignore that content. Also, any emotions we experience will feel stronger because they are unexpected. In subsequent plays, we will expect the arc of the game and thus our emotional experience may be more muted. If the majority of the thematic experience relies on surface level theme and novelty, the theme likely will fade faster in subsequent plays.

There are many other reasons for why thematic disengagement happens. As I am not a psychologist, I can only speak to processes that are within a designer's control. So, let us look at ways to improve the lifespan of thematic engagement rather than trying to settle the exact causes of disengagement.

Thematic Efficiency

Make the efficient strategy thematic. The main axiom of theme fade seems to be that players who are engaged with theme will play suboptimally and as they become disengaged will shift to more optimal play. On the one hand, I think that suboptimal game play should always be fun and that theme can be a source of that fun. On the other hand, why can't the efficient play be thematic as well? If optimal play causes total disengagement with the theme, I have to wonder how well-knitted the theme is with gameplay to begin with. There are some games where it would be difficult to totally disengage with the theme, such as racing games like *Flamme Rouge*, where the efficient play (making use of slipstreams and only pulling ahead at the end) is the thematic play. In order to make efficiency feel thematic, the win condition must be the thematic core, and the rest of the elements need to align with it.

Thematic Labels

Get players to speak in thematic terms. Speaking of thematic alignment, the words players speak while playing will drive engagement with the theme. Thematic terms need to be accessible and useful to players in order for players to use them. In a racing game, players will probably use terms like "finish line" automatically. However, many games use unintuitive language for components. Your product design will affect whether players refer to the components by their color or a more thematic term. Refer back to the discussion in Chapter 2 on baked-in and opt-in elements.

Board game design is all about crafting how players will use and experience your game. One aspect to pay attention to is how players speak and describe what they are doing during gameplay. If the language isn't thematic, the game experience likely isn't either.

Thematic Emotions

Continuing our focus on thematic alignment, *player emotions should fit with the experience the theme provides.* This is often touted as a way to avoid ludonarrative dissonance, but there is another reason.[9] When you watch a horror movie, feeling scared deepens your experience of the movie. When players feel emotions that make sense for their avatar in the game, that deepens their experience of the game. These emotions feed back into the theme and can serve as a thematic reminder to experienced players of why they should care about the theme. I have touched on player experience, but it is largely outside of the scope of this book.

Thematic Framing

Provide a clear narrative framework. Of course, the easiest way (I think it's cheating) to maintain thematic engagement is to make a narrative-driven game. Forcing players to engage with a written narrative keeps their focus on the theme, even when the mechanics are unthematic. However, we can do similar things by providing a clear narrative framework with our mechanics and win conditions. By telling players who they are and what they want, we allow them to become invested in the game world. If we then give them mechanics that flow logically from the game world we have established, we can co-create a narrative with our players. Refer back to Chapter 5 for more on how to frame your narrative.

Minimal Math

Lastly, *pay attention to the amount of calculation in the game.* When players are spending a lot of time analyzing all possible moves, they are likely less engaged with the theme. While certain amounts of calculation will not detract from theme (and certain themes can align with calculation), narrative and calculation tend to be one or the other for our brains. When I am doing math I cannot also think about my avatar's desires and struggles. One solution is to alternate moments of math with narrative or to provide narrative checkpoints during game pauses. Another solution is to make the calculation "in character" for the avatar. Finally, you can minimize calculation, which has a side benefit of speeding up gameplay.

By integrating theme at all levels of gameplay, designers can offer players richer experiences that unfold over multiple plays, where surface theme gives way to deeper mechanical theming. This allows players to explore the theme, perhaps moving back and forth between optimal and suboptimal strategies from play to play.

Exercise 11.1: Pick one of your own designs. List out the elements that provide a sense of familiarity to players. List any twists. Try to identify if there is too much thematic detail, especially during your game explanation.

Exercise 11.2: Pick one of your own designs or a published game. Is the efficient play thematic? How would the theme need to change to make efficiency fit better with the theme?

NOTES

1. This is the formula I developed to explain what makes a game resonate. This formula is inspired by the concepts in *Made to Stick: Why Some Ideas Survive and Others Die* by Chip and Dan Heath. (Chip Heath and Dan Heath, *Made to Stick: Why Some Ideas Survive and Others Die*. New York: Random House, 2007.) They developed the "SUCCESs" model, which stands for Simple, Unexpected, Concrete, Credible, Emotions, and Stories. It is a handy mnemonic, but the authors admit that it doesn't show the relationship that exists between the traits they outline. I reworked the model to show interconnectedness and cut the element (credible) that is mostly outside the scope of design. (Internal credibility can be built within a piece of entertainment or art through the use of vivid details that support the core idea. I'm proposing that by following my formula for resonance, you will produce this feeling in players anyway, so including this trait would ultimately be redundant. Internal Credibility is the product of resonance, not a cause, and external credibility is outside the scope of this discussion.)
2. Knitted themes and evocative actions are discussed in Chapter 2.
3. The term fantasy is discussed further in Chapter 8.
4. Research is discussed further in Chapter 10.
5. Often, what is applauded as innovative are small changes that are well implemented.
6. If you are including an unnecessary element that you don't think is cool, why are you doing that? Don't do that.
7. Some people view gimmicks as marketing hooks, but I refer to those aspects of a product as hooks.
8. Stephen Blessing and Elena Sakosky, interview with Geoffrey Engelstein, "GameTek 213.5—The Incan Gold Experiment," Ludology, podcast audio, November 24, 2019, https://ludology.libsyn.com/gametek-2135-the-incan-gold-experiment.
9. Recall that ludonarrative dissonance is a term used when the stated narrative of a game and the gameplay experience are in conflict with each other.

REFERENCES

1. Heath, Chip and Dan Heath. *Made to Stick: Why Some Ideas Survive and Others Die*. New York: Random House, 2007.
2. Blessing, Stephen and Elena Sakosky. Interview with Geoffrey Engelstein. "GameTek 213.5-The Incan Gold Experiment." *Ludology*. Podcast audio. November 24, 2019. https://ludology.libsyn.com/gametek-2135-the-incan-gold-experiment.

GAMES REFERENCED

Four Gardens
Caverna
Agricola
The Grizzled
The Coldest Night
Flamme Rouge

CHAPTER 12

Design Reference Guides

THIS CHAPTER CONSISTS OF several guides to get you using the concepts discussed in this book. The first guide takes you from the idea stage through a first draft. The second guide focuses on retheming an existing design. The third guide is a checklist to make sure you don't go overboard with theme.

DESIGN PROCESS QUICK GUIDE

There is no one right way to design a thematic game. Many of the steps outlined in Chapters 3–11 can be rearranged in an order that suits your preferred process. I have divided the topics into three stages as a suggestion for how to move forward with development.

Scaffolding—Research, Metaphors, Structures, and Vision

The concept of scaffolding is that it is the preliminary structural shape around which you can grow your theme. Designs usually start with a simple idea. From that idea, you can do some preliminary research and decide what you want to model in your design. You can refine that idea into a central metaphor and/or settle on a mechanical structure that could best support that metaphor. During this process, think about the type of experience you want players to have and write a design vision statement.

These concepts are laid out in Chapters 3 and 10.

Outline—Goals, Obstacles, and Actions

Once your scaffolding is in place, it's time to think about the broad strokes of how your game will work mechanically and thematically. Figure out

DOI: 10.1201/9781003453765-15

what the players' goals are, what keeps them from achieving their goals, and what consequences there are for failure and success. Then consider what types of actions can mechanically represent what is happening in the theme. Now is a good time for more significant research in order to gain the knowledge needed to effectively abstract the theme as you begin to develop the mechanics.

These concepts are discussed in Chapter 4.

Details—Plot, Character, and Setting

As development of mechanics continues, pay attention to narrative framing to keep the scope of the theme limited to what exists during gameplay. Develop your plot, characters, and setting. As you playtest, edit your theme to increase player engagement. As you get closer to pitching or publication, work on the thematic hook. If you have put in the work, the thematic hook should be both obvious and punchy.

The thematic hook of a game (aka the answer to the question "what is the theme?") is best defined by this formula: "Noun + Verb + Win Condition + ?". Themes should have verbs, should be tied to the win condition of a game, and should be able to be phrased as questions.

These concepts are discussed in Chapters 5–8 and 11.

You can speed run most of the first two stages in a single evening. However, you'll probably have to revisit the outline stage for additional research. There is also an important stage that occurs concurrently with the third stage where you will be iterating design concepts and playtesting. You may go long stretches of time without working on your theme. Reference your scaffolding to keep the game in line with your vision when you add new systems, but remember that you will have to sacrifice some thematic rigor to achieve ease of play.

GUIDE TO RETHEMING A GAME

What do you do when your initial idea for a game does not include a theme or if you have to retheme? Below is a guide for attaching a theme to existing mechanics:

- *Ask interesting questions.* Interrogating your design involves asking interesting questions. If the answers you get are not interesting, chances are the questions you are asking aren't either. You don't want just any theme; you want an interesting theme.

- *Identify one element.* Decide what one resource or card type is. Which is to say, don't theme your whole game first; theme one bit of it. The element you theme should spark ideas for the rest of the game. In other words, the element you theme first should be interesting. If the rest of this exercise doesn't yield a good direction to build out a theme, reset to this point and start over.
- *Find the movement.* How do you make a single element interesting? Find the elements that move during gameplay and pick one. I'm assuming that your initial idea for a game included enough mechanics to play at least half of one turn. Which pieces moved physically? Of those pieces, which piece moves in the most interesting way? Theme that piece first. Why does that piece move that way? Find the most satisfying explanation and you'll have a good start on your theme. Not every game has to have pieces that move in thematic ways, but this is a good exercise to generate theme even if you end up moving away from your initial concept.
- *Build out your theme.* Now that you have one thematic element, figure out what the rest are. This should be fairly easy if your initial element really resonated with you. If not, you can always return to the previous step and continue brainstorming. Identify each element in a way that makes your initial element more interesting. If your design shifts focus to a new "most interesting element," build out the theme around that element instead. You also need to decide what roles the players assume during play at this stage. That includes the characters' motivations—why they want to be performing the actions that make up the game.
- *Find the relationships.* As you are building out your theme, establish how the elements are related to one another. If the names of your resources could be easily swapped out for their colors and players wouldn't notice, your resources don't have thematic relationships to each other. It is easier to remember that wheat turns into flour than that brown cubes turn into white; so if your playtesters aren't using your resources names, it is likely because they aren't really thematic.[1]
- *Identify the boring bits and troubleshoot.* Play your game and focus only on the theme. Did you care all the way through? Which parts

were you less invested in? Did you care about your avatar? Did you care about the NPCs? If you built something, did it feel important to you? It's easy at this stage to blame the boring bits on the unrefined mechanics. Approach this stage with the aim to make the story your game tells better. You may end up essentially re-retheming the game at this stage. That is a normal part of development. If a mechanic were to no longer work in your game, you would cut it and replace it. Think about theme the same way. Keep what is interesting and toss what isn't. One way to know if you are on the right track is if your elevator pitch gets shorter and punchier. (Test your elevator pitch. There's plenty of online forums that will give feedback. In the process, you are covertly testing your theme.) Be aware, this step is an ongoing process as you playtest and tweak your mechanics.

WHEN TO DIAL BACK THEME

This section originally appeared in Cardboard Edison's *Best Practices* guide for 2023.[2]

Theme can greatly enhance the experience of play. When well-executed, theme can make rules intuitive, set players' expectations prior to play, provide atmosphere during play, and encourage creative play over efficient play. Theme should provide moments of discovery for players. However, *too much* theme can detract and distract from gameplay. Here are a few places where you can afford to dial back your theme:

- *The rulebook.* First and foremost, players must be able to learn your game. Theme should increase accessibility of rules, not decrease it. Start by writing a rulebook with as little extra worldbuilding as possible, then add just enough theme that the rules become more intuitive and memorable. But remember, the rulebook is a manual for play, not a work of fiction.
- *Story summaries.* Your theme should be about what occurs during gameplay. Don't tell players in a lore paragraph that the story is about smuggling when the game is actually about haggling. You may have a really cool story, but if it doesn't inform gameplay, it doesn't belong in the game. This may include character backstories that don't make sense and are only included for comedic purposes, but your mileage may vary.

- *Naming conventions.* Simple nouns are usually fine, but proper nouns of fictional places, people, or things will create terminology confusion. Limit your terms to (at most) one hard to pronounce, unintuitive word. "Store" is always acceptable, but "discorporate" is a bridge too far, especially if you also have "immolate" and "Zargoblastia" as terms in your game. Playtesters will use helpful terms and skip confusing ones, so listen to them during play.
- *Decisions made by the player, not their avatar.* Don't theme decisions such as which player color to choose, which map to start on, etc. In-world decisions generally only occur during player turns. Setup, cleanup, and bookkeeping can have some theme, but a light hand is necessary.
- *When one detail creates unintended implications.* If you have a group of meeples and one is in a skirt, the implication becomes that that one is female and the rest are not. Whereas having all generic meeples can be seen as genderless.
- *Too many thematic details, in general.* Declutter your theme. Too many thematic details can obscure the story you are trying to tell. A named character signals a different level of importance than an unnamed character, but if they are all named, players may not be able to distinguish which characters are worth investing in.
- *Details that tell players how to feel.* Adjectives like scary or surprising are not thematic, but rather attempts to tell players what kind of experience they should be having. This is a classic case of Show; Don't Tell. Provide the experience and let players discover it for themselves.

Theme is like salt. The right amount can make a dish sing, but too much ruins the soup. Theme should never impede gameplay, but should reinforce the intended play experience.

Exercise 12.1: Pick one of your design ideas and go through as much of the process described in the quick guide as you can in two hours.

Exercise 12.2: Pick a published game. Using the steps in this chapter, come up with a new theme for the game.

Exercise 12.3: Pick a published thematic game. Identify where the theme got in the way of the game.

NOTES

1. Science Fiction themed games run into this problem regularly with fictional technology. Even fictional gadgets should have explainable purposes that make sense to players within the context of the game world.
2. https://cardboardedison.com/award

REFERENCE

1. https://cardboardedison.com/award.

CHAPTER 13

Conclusion

Plenty of excellent designers design intuitively, without any formal training. In any art form, if you know what works, you don't necessarily need to know why in order to perform a given technique. So, why learn theory at all? Board game design has been chugging along since the nineties mostly through design iteration and oral tradition. When is it important to know why something works?

I believe that formalized knowledge (and, to an extent, formal training) makes for more competent practitioners who can work more efficiently. Chefs who understand the real reason behind a technique are better equipped to alter a recipe or make adjustments to a technique in order to make something that is both new and tasty. Knowing what the technique is actually doing makes it easier to change or replace. Better understanding of what a mechanism is accomplishing means zeroing in on what could replace it with fewer false starts. I think designers generally understand this concept even if they've never thought about it explicitly.

Where we get tripped up is in believing that some knowledge is ineffable. Belief that certain things can only be learned by years of experience (or by lucking into something that works) does two things. First, it trains us to believe that inefficiency is a feature, not a bug. In other words, that the years of grinding away are a necessary part of the process before we can produce anything of quality. Experience is important, but we can level up our skills in a number of ways. Second, ignoring formal knowledge stops us from exploring concepts that appear on the outside to be abstract or ethereal. Exploring abstract concepts helps us think more flexibly.

DOI: 10.1201/9781003453765-16

Flexible thinking makes us better designers. And that's before we account for the benefit of learning the abstract concepts themselves.

I firmly believe that there are any number of concepts that are extremely helpful to absorb then sort of forget. Once you understand the principles, you don't need to remember what they are called. You will simply know how something "should" be done. Certain concepts can be recalled specifically when troubleshooting, but are more often utilized instinctively when creating. (This is also why you can skip formal learning, but it takes longer to figure out what works through trial and error.) The concepts laid out in this book trend toward that foundational sort of theory, the kind you are meant to forget. Think of these concepts as an optical illusion that once you begin to see them a certain way, you cannot go back to your initial confusion. This is the type of theory that teaches you not what to do but how to see.

Why learn theory? Because it will make you a better designer, and you never know what bits you learn will end up being useful down the road. And if you learn something that doesn't stick, well, that's okay. There isn't going to be a test.

Index

Note: *Italic* page numbers refer to figures.

For Product Safety Concerns and Information please contact our EU representative GPSR@taylorandfrancis.com
Taylor & Francis Verlag GmbH, Kaufingerstraße 24, 80331 München, Germany

www.ingramcontent.com/pod-product-compliance
Ingram Content Group UK Ltd.
Pitfield, Milton Keynes, MK11 3LW, UK
UKHW021433080625
459435UK00011B/258
9781032584058